Designing Organizations for the Betterment of Society

"Rodrigo Magalhães' book stimulates students and scholars of management and organization to understand organizational designing in a new light, where ethics is deeply linked to aesthetics and creative aspects."

—Antonio Strati, *Dept. of Sociology & Social Research, University of Trento*

"By prioritizing morality, collaboration, and purpose over material and instrumental concerns, this book develops a human-centered design approach. Magalhães argues that the field of Management and Organization Studies must include a concern for ethics and aesthetics if it wishes to help organizations contribute to the betterment of society."

—Charles Snow, *Professor Emeritus, Penn State University*

Rodrigo Magalhães

Designing Organizations for the Betterment of Society

The Ethic-Aesthetic Scaffold

palgrave
macmillan

Rodrigo Magalhães
Kuwait College of Science
and Technology
Kuwait, Kuwait

ISBN 978-3-031-64482-5 ISBN 978-3-031-64483-2 (eBook)
https://doi.org/10.1007/978-3-031-64483-2

This Palgrave Macmillan imprint is published by the registered company Springer Nature Switzerland AG
The registered company address is: Gewerbestrasse 11, 6330 Cham, Switzerland

Preface

After my PhD studies in Organizational Information Systems, at the London School of Economics, and throughout my post-PhD career, I have always felt that something is missing in the connection between IT and the organization. Then, after years of researching and debating the problem from many points of view, I have come to the conclusion that organization design is the missing piece. IT is just part of the artefacts that make up organization design, but quite a major part, because when IT changes, the organization's design changes. This seems to indicate that the level at which to tackle the consequences of IT is indeed the level of organization design, and if this is the case the new questions can be asked. We see the growth of the digital, the opportunities it creates the profits it brings, but we do not see the benefits in terms of the societal and environmental problems the world is grappling with. In other words, how can we harness the power of the digital for the common good?

On the other hand, we, MOS (Management and Organization Studies) researchers go on, oblivious of some of the most serious crises that the world has seen regarding the environment, social inequality, public health and even threats to democracy. Is there a role for us, and for organization design in particular? Organization design does have a role, if it is agreed that everything that happens in the organization has to be designed, and that designing the organization *in its entirety* falls within the remit of our responsibilities, as a professional group. Organizational purpose seems to be a good place to start the process. In managerial circles, purpose is usually understood as the organization's vision and mission; however, experience shows that rosy vision/mission statements on most websites, endless promises of generous stakeholder inclusion, well-intentioned plans for doing good for the poor and pledges of good governance, have produced negligible results, as well as shaky credibility for many.

Thus, the solution seems to lie at a level *above* organizational purpose, that is, a meta level. This is something that has been suggested by design scholars as part of the paradigmatic shift known as "meta-designing" and described as a major challenge faced by the design discipline in the Anthropocene (Wood, 2022). In organization studies, some writers have anticipated this shift, using designations such as "platform" or "virtual organizing scheme" (Ciborra 1996), "meta-capability" (Snow et al. 2005) or "design gestalt" (Yoo et al., 2006) to describe organization design. Some unorthodox writers have suggested that organization design should be seen as a cultural construction (Clegg 1994; Bate et al. 2000), thus reinforcing the meta-level conceptualization. In this book, I stand on the shoulders of these pioneers, and try to put meat on the bones of the concepts of platform, meta-capability and design gestalt, while going beyond the symbolic understanding of culture, and introducing practices, aesthetics and ethics, as the non-representational[1] components of organizational life.

If organization design can be seen as a *supra-organizational* force, with ethic and aesthetic overtones, this would mean a 180° turn in relation to the old school, where organization design was about contingency, fit, structure or configuration. The new approach places the spotlight on a new conception of the organization designer, as a managerial incumbency aimed at building/looking after the organization's ethic-aesthetic scaffold and making it thrive. The scaffold is built from the bottom, where artefacts (including IT), as well as the interactions, relationships and experiences of people need to conform to the letter and the spirit of a newly

[1] Oxford Reference.com (2024) provides the following entry: "Non-representational theorists consider how researchers might 'represent' what they encounter in their fieldwork, since, they argue, 'representational' theory generates an unwavering, deadened picture of the world. They emphasize knowing through connection and participation; the spotlight is on the process, rather than the outcome—'it ain't what you get but the way that you got it'. This means that academics have to move beyond mere representation". The expression "non-representational theory" has been used by several writers in MOS (Beyes and Steyaert 2012; Gherardi 2017; Juhlin and Holt 2022; Vitry et al. 2020).

inspired kind of organization purpose. This, I suggest, is the way to make organizations contribute to the betterment of society.

Kuwait Rodrigo Magalhães

Acknowledgments

I would like to express my gratitude to Khalid Al-Begain, Antonio Strati, John Dobson, Charles Snow and Tom Wilson for the support and advice.

References

Barry, D. 2011. Re-designing Organization Design. Paper presented at the Design Business Conference, Barcelona, November 17–18.

Beyes, T., and C. Steyaert. 2012. Spacing Organization: Non-representational Theory and Performing Organizational Space. *Organization* 19 (1): 45–61.

Ciborra, C.U. 1996. The Platform Organization: Recombining Strategies, Structures and Surprises. *Organization Science* 7: 103–118.

Clegg, S. 1994. Weber and Foucault: Social Theory for the Study of Organizations. *Organization* 1 (1): 149–178.

Gherardi, S. 2016. To Start Practice Theorizing A new: The Contribution of the Concepts of Agencement and Formativeness. *Organization* 23 (5): 680–698.

Juhlin, C., and Holt, R. 2022. The sensory imperative. *Management Learning*, 53 (4): 640–651 https://doi.org/10.1177/13505076211062220

Snow, C.C., R.E. Miles, and G. Miles. 2005. A Configurational Approach to the Integration of Strategy and Organization Research. *Strategic Organization* 3 (4): 431–439.

Vitry, C.; Sage, D. and Dainty, A. 2020. Affective atmospheres of sensemaking and learning: workplace meetings as aesthetic and anaesthetic. *Management Learning*, 51 (3): 274–292

Wood, J. 2022. *Metadesigning: Designing in the Anthropocene*. New York: Routledge

Contents

List of Figures

List of Tables

CHAPTER 1

Introduction

Abstract This chapter starts by highlighting that contingency-led thinking, the dominant school of thought, has had a reductionist effect on the understanding of what organization design is, so that in managerial circles organization design continues to mean a simple formula for efficiency-seeking and profit-maximizing performance, oblivious of anything to do with the ethical, environmental or social consequences of the organization's activity. In the last couple of decades, there has been a growing trend aimed at bringing design closer to management, with management being depicted as a practice that goes beyond decision-making and plays an active role in the ongoing design of the organization. This trend has begun a shift in organization design from what organizations "are" to what they "could be", with a focus on warmer, livelier and more engaging approaches, incorporating the sensory, aesthetic and ethical sides of design. Building on this background, the book proposes a new framework with a solid normative foundation, built primarily on the principles of morality and humanism from the design discipline and highlighting a *new managerial responsibility*—holistic organization designing. This managerial responsibility is complementary of strategic management, in the sense that the designing role is also required to assess and evaluate organizational performance but using a new type of yardstick—sensory/aesthetic/experiential—in addition to the regular rational and instrumental measures.

R. Magalhães, *Designing Organizations for the Betterment of Society*,
https://doi.org/10.1007/978-3-031-64483-2_1

Keywords Design discipline · Holistic · Humanism · Managerial responsibility · Morality · Organization design

> Although economic measures are often used to determine inequality, it is also necessary to consider the ways in which social structures, including organizations, are *designed* and/or evolve to advantage some groups over others (…) Our purpose in this editorial is to call for us – a community of engaged management scholars – to take inequality seriously because organizations are centrally implicated in the reification of societal inequalities. (Amis et al. 2021, italics added)

> Increase in the magnitude and the complexity of moral behaviour is first the result of increased *specialization*, especially in economic activities and in the machinery and materials which are employed for materialistic purposes. Attention is increasingly given to the technical knowledge now required and to the technical skills arising from specialized experience. The moral factor involved in these activities seems to be almost entirely neglected. (Barnard 1958: 12, italics added)

> The key words of the modernist business universe of the past 150 years may have been those of logic, reason, science, technical expertise, instrumental rationality, wealth maximization, and moral rectitude. But the key concepts of the *aesthetic business* era will be such things as harmony, balance, sustainability, aesthetic excellence, judgment, context, compassion, community, beauty, and art. Those corporate cultures that recognize this shift will flourish both financially and aesthetically and will genuinely contribute to quality of life. (Dobson 2007: 45, italics added)

The first citation above, from an editorial note in the Association of Management Review, serves as a reminder that organizations not just evolve but they are also intentionally designed, and that *design* has many consequences. The second citation comes from a little-known paper by Chester Barnard published in the California Management Review and drawing our attention to the fact that the issue of business morals contained within organizations as social artefacts seems to be slipping out of control, mostly due to the technical knowledge and the unbridled deployment of *material artefacts*, which have dominated the organizational landscape for the last 65 years. Essentially, the two articles highlight with great clarity the apparent inability of organization and management scholar or practitioners to propose, prescribe or adopt the ***morality*** and the ***designs*** that are needed to harness the technology and the extraordinary efficiency gains it provides for curbing social inequality, global warming, toxic workplaces, dishonest corporate governance and the multitude of ills that affect us all as members of society. The third citation, by John Dobson, brings a degree of hope, talking about a new era of ***aesthetic business***, and painting a scenario for the future of management and inherently for the future of organization design.

Unlike other disciplines, management does not have to follow a deontological code, and in most organizations, it is unclear where the responsibility lies for issues of a moral or ethical nature. Organization design would seem to be a candidate for a focal point on organizational ethics; however, organization design does not have an obvious role in terms of regular organizational functioning, and although some see it as being at the core of many contemporary organizational ills, interest in organization design as an academic topic has waned dramatically over the years. The reasons for this demise are manifold. Firstly, the definitions and intellectual approaches behind organization design theory date back to the industrial age and are no longer relevant today. Secondly, contingency-led thinking has had a reductionist effect on the understanding of what organization design is (Van de Ven et al. 2014), so that in managerial circles organization design continues to mean a simple formula for efficiency-seeking and profit maximizing performance, oblivious of anything to do with the ethical, environmental or social consequences of the organization's activity. Thirdly, as a scholarly area, organization design receives little or no input from design as the discipline dealing with the creation of artefacts (Simon 1996), a lacuna that has implications for the way we think about the social responsibility of management. Indeed, this is part and parcel of a broader trend in management and organization studies (MOS), where morality continues to be "a victim of [the] endeavor of business academics to make management a science" (Ghoshal 2005: 79).

The reductionism imposed by the traditional approach has several profound and long-lasting consequences. Firstly, the principle of hierarchy, upon which much of organizational theory was built, dates back to a time when environments, as well as organizational structures, could be classified as stable. With the advent of the information age, globalization and the knowledge economy, the relationship between organizational structures and their surroundings has changed beyond recognition. Secondly, the development of digital infrastructures in all types of organizations has led to a subversion of hierarchical rules and to a dramatic loss of relevance of the traditional precepts of organizational design. This has created new challenges in terms of the form and content of organizational interactions and relationships, which have not yet been systematically theorized (Zammuto et al. 2007). Thirdly, the contingency-dominated approach maintains the misleading assumption that organizational design refers only to the macro level of organizational structure, with a rigid separation between the formal and informal organizations (McEvily et al. 2014). However, despite the many studies that show that informal organization is as important or more important than formal organization, and that the principles of hierarchy and unity of command are not as relevant as they were in the industrial era, the teaching of organizational design still remains unchanged.

In reflecting upon the reasons why the traditional approach(es) to organization design have not produced results that can credibly advance organization theory, Weick (2004: 40) suggests five erroneous beliefs, which lie at that at root of the problem: (i) the presumption of a central designer, (ii) alignment with formal authority, (iii) the organization as a material entity, (iv) the prescribed rather than the emergent and (v) choices rather than construction. To these, a sixth point could be added to express the lack of a ***normative ambition*** about designing with aesthetic and moral values. And herein lies the problem which has impeded organization design from becoming a more effective MOS construct: *the status of "design"* in organization design. We posit that this problem will not be solved until "design" is detached from its current status as a metaphor and is allowed to assume a *foundational role* in organization (design) theory. In practice, this means allowing organizations to be seen as objects of design and considering in their theorizing, the principles from the design discipline, including the domain of design ethics.

The Trend Towards Generativity, Self-Organization and Humanism

In the last couple of decades, there has been a growing trend aimed at bringing design closer to management, with management being depicted as a practice that goes beyond decision-making and plays an active role in the ongoing design of the organization (Boland and Collopy 2004; Van Aken 2004; Van Aken and Romme 2009). And in one of the most recent calls for a new paradigm for organization design, Snow and Fjeldstat (2024) reinforce the point that the focus needs to change from structure to the "means that enable goal-directed self-organizing" (ibid.: xvii). Thus, rather than a linear and material process of setting up organizational structures, organization design is conceptualized as a virtual (Ciborra 1996), circular (Romme and Endenburg 2006), morphing as a whole (Rindova and Kotha 2001; Yoo et al. 2006) and never-ending (Boland et al. 2008; Dunbar et al. 2008; Garud et al. 2008) process of designing, driven by not only technical-structural rules but also generative ones (Garud et al. 2006; Parrish 2010). And rather than being determined by the environment, designs are now seen as capable of shaping and even creating new environments (Sarasvathy et al. 2008). An offshoot of this trend develops a perspective focused on the human aspects of design (Avital et al. 2006; Avital and Te'eni 2009) and the idea that organization design should be aimed at shaping hopeful organizations, with positive experiences for stakeholders. This is pursued by Jelinek et al. (2008) in urging organization design researchers to adopt a design science approach, asking questions about what organizations "could be", rather than what they "are", and focusing on how their research might lead to "the betterment of the human condition" (ibid.: 317). Barry (2011), on the other hand, predicts "a shift in organizational design thinking towards a warmer, livelier, and more engaging field that incorporates the sensory, aesthetic, artful, and creative sides of design" (cited in Van de Ven et al. 2014: 417).

Although rich in analytical content, this trend has not succeeded in debunking the traditional emphases of organization design on structure and hierarchy, or in taking the topic into new directions of ethics or morality. Unlike other professional groups, such as medicine or the law, the communities behind MOS have opted to remain neutral on issues of moral conduct, or quality of life, in spite of the many voices that have, over the years, called for a change in the status quo. One of these voices was Russell Ackoff's (1981), who, more than four decades ago, urged corporations to assume a posture of moral responsibility for their stakeholders, including the quality of life and the personal/professional development of their members, instead of the more comfortable and mechanistic stance of no responsibility for their purpose. Not long after, the proponents of stakeholder theory initiate a powerful campaign for a normative approach to management and for a recognition of the moral character of managerial action (Freeman 1984; Donaldson and Preston 1995; Harrison et al. 2019). More recently, ESG (environmental, social and governance) concerns have resurfaced, in response to the global warming, social inequalities and the COVID crisis, with calls from academia for corporations to rethink and reform the way they perceive, articulate and implement their purpose (George et al. 2023; Nonaka and Takeuchi 2021).

The Challenges

But despite such efforts, the unfortunate reality is that the worth of organizational purpose as recorded in public statements of mission or vision, is still perceived as being a little more than exercises in public relations. Nonetheless, most statements of organizational purpose are filled with good intentions as regards the fulfilment of the organization's social and environmental responsibilities, and to be fair, many top management teams are sincere about their intentions. The problem is that in attempting to fulfil promises and expectations, myriad obstacles get in the way and most of these are due to *legacy factors*, which can be divided into two categories: people-related and artefact-related. People-related factors refer to "ways of doing things", which have worked well in the past and any kind of attempted change is swamped with difficulties. Artefact-related factors concern the way artefacts have been designed and/or implemented, and they can also present formidable obstacles to change. Special reference is made to the new digital artefacts and the many ways in which they seem to have acquired "a will of its own", with serious moral, social, environmental and economic consequences. This combination of human and material factors lies at the bottom of organization design as a management and organizational problem. Moreover, as stated before, organization design theory is devoid of markers of a moral or ethical nature, arguably one of the reasons for the relative lack of social responsibility on the part of management.

If we now assume that the essence of (organization) design is the creation and management of (organizational) artefacts and if we believe that organization design is more than organizational structure, and that all the outcomes of organizational action are the result of design- and people-related decisions, then, organizational purpose emerges as the beginning and the end of *all* design- and people-related decisions taken in/by the organization, and the starting point for the practice and the theory of organization design. As hinted at before, such a theory should be inspired by the precepts of the design discipline and as such the pragmatic and normative ambitions of design would also have an effect on organizational purpose and its execution. Thus, while urging for a radical re-rethink of the foundations of a topic that is still of great intellectual worth, we see the need to provide organization design with an approach that is inspired by values of morality and humanity but at the same time aligned with the institutional realities of organizations.

The New Approach

In line with the complexity of the organizational phenomenon, the topic of organization design is necessarily multifaceted, requiring a highly diversified approach. A good example of such complexity and diversification can be found in one of our key sources Shrivastava et al. (2017),—an article on the topic of sustainability, published in *The Journal of Applied Behavioural Science*, and touching on topics as diverse as design thinking, organizational ethics, decision-making, strategy, aesthetics and virtue ethics. We follow this source in its efforts to highlight the need for organization studies to combine the traditional instrumental rationality of organizational thinking with aesthetic rationality. The authors' contention, and ours, is that this combination will provide a more comprehensive picture of how rationality operates in organizational settings and that it could even "qualitatively open new spatiality and temporality in organizations" (ibid.: 378). The article also builds on the new awareness created by design thinking about the fact that design is a way to add "the beauty" into products, services and organizational processes, and that aesthetic enhancements can inform managerial policies through values such as compassion, social justice, care for the environment and community.

Against this background, and acutely aware of the need for a solid normative foundation, the new approach builds primarily on the principles of morality and humanism from the design discipline (Bonsiepe 2006; Krippendorff 2006; Manzini 2015). These highlight the fundamentally ethical nature of human-centred design and claim that any design creation affects somebody (or many people) and therefore no design should be carried out without the participation of the stakeholders. The framework is also underpinned by the belief that organization design is the outcome of the *co-evolution* of two different paradigms: the paradigm of organization as something intentionally planned, formally structured and designed on the basis of stable representations, versus the paradigm of organization as something essentially emergent, informally structured, led by an organically grown set of rules and not amenable to representation in space or time. In other words, organization design as the result of the co-evolution of two types of organizational mechanisms: structure and culture (Bate et al. 2000).

Authors, such as Kimberly (1984), Clegg (1994) or Ciborra (1996) have pointed out that the study of organization design must include people and culture; however, culture is usually left out of discussions on organization design, because it is perceived as a generic set of abstract or mentalistic representations of organizational life, difficult to apply in practice. Our approach, however, is rooted on the notion that the meanings that make up the organization's design are much more than cultural symbols, and include also the emotions, feelings and sensations of everyday events. This is part of the so-called non-representational turn in the social sciences (Reckwitz 2012; Thrift 2008) which coalesces around the topics of organizational ethics (Shrivastava et al. 2017) and aesthetics (Baldessarelli et al. 2022). Accordingly, cultural phenomena are also aesthetic in nature, and they encompass not only representations such as symbols, but also pre-cognitive manifestations of meaning, such as feelings, emotions and affects. A cultural-ethic-aesthetic approach to organization design addresses the poor reductionist legacy inherited from the conventional approach and responds to the call by organization design scholars, such as Van de Ven et al. (2014), for new conceptual frameworks "that avoid such a reductionist quagmire and begin to address organization systems from a more *holistic* perspective" (ibid.: 403, italics added).

Aesthetics offers a rich epistemological framework for description and research into organization design without resorting to the oversimplification of the complexity of the organizational phenomenon. It offers a new perspective into the making of meaning in organizations (Taylor and Hansen 2005) and as such it is closely connected with the foundational notion from human-centred design that *to design is to establish meaning* (Krippendorff 1989). This design trend has found its way into the management literature through the work of Verganti (2009, 2016), where meaning is highlighted as the driver of business innovation; however, Verganti's approach has not been applied to the myriad of *organizational artefacts* that make up a large portion of the organization's design in the eyes of internal and external stakeholders.

It is obvious that organizations cannot be designed in the same way that we design buildings, bridges, public parks or software programs. The artefacts that make up the organizational infrastructure can be planned and designed and there are multiple methodologies for doing so, but the organization as a holistic sociomaterial artefact cannot be determined or pre-planned. However, in considering the organization as a whole, there is an opportunity to influence its moral direction by focusing on the ethic-aesthetics implications of organizational artefacts, and on the ensuing consequences on organizational interactions, relationships and experiences, in line with the organization's purpose. This is our proposal of organization design as an ethic-aesthetic scaffold.

The New Organization Design Model

The repositioning of organization design theory proposed in this book is depicted in a model inspired by several sources from MOS and design theory. From MOS, one of the important sources is Barnard (1938), which may seem a rather anachronistic choice; however, although "often barely acknowledged" (Pye 1994: 1125), we find that Barnard is still one of the most pragmatic and insightful of all management writers, proven by the frequency of citations to his work. Based on Barnard's suggestion that the final efficiency of organization depends on two different modes of organizing—a core managerial activity of controlling costs, output and income, versus "the creative economy of the whole" (ibid.: 253)—we suggest that organization design follows a similar logic. Therefore, we recommend that organization design should also be split into the two levels of analysis: the operational/technical/local and the holistic level.

The technical level of localized organization design is the focus of a great deal of specialized methodological frameworks for the design and implementation of organizational artefacts, developed by both academic researchers and management consultants. Although they are not part of the traditional definitions of organization design, it must be recognized that organizational artefacts play a major role in the overall shaping of the organization, affecting not only its internal functioning, but also the *experience* that stakeholders have of its operations, as well as its image and even its reputation. Due to the large number of subject areas covered and the highly specialized nature of such frameworks, this level of organization design will not be examined in any detail in this book. Thus, the bulk of our book is dedicated to the holistic level of organization design, in a formulation that is entirely original in the context of MOS. This proposal emerges, on one hand, in response to the need for an organizational tool that can present a coherent and organization-wide answer to the moral crisis associated with the social and environmental challenges that organizations currently face. On the other hand, our proposal is also a reflection of the need to ensure that technological artefacts are placed at the service of organizational purpose, and do not serve as excuses for exceptions or deviations.

The organization design model comprises three components. The first explores non-representational epistemology in an attempt to answer the question "what theoretical approach should we use to study organization design"? Accordingly, organization design is depicted as a highly dynamic process of change driven by the artefact-mediated daily actions of organizational members. Two types of non-representational tools are adopted: social practice and aesthetic analysis.

The second component of the model provides the normative background and attempts to answer the question "what normative considerations should drive organization design(ing)?" This component is based on a triad made up by morality, collaboration and purpose, originally inspired by Barnard's theory of organization but brought up to date through the recent work of various authors (Baldessarelli et al. 2022; Bernacchio et al. 2022; George et al. 2023), to include MacIntyre's (2007) approach to virtue ethics and Dobson's (2004, 2010, 2022) merger of organizational aesthetics with the morality of virtue ethics.

The third component expounds the hypothesis of organization design-as-meaning and attempts to answer the ontological question "what is organization design" under the assumption that organization design can be defined as a perception or set of meanings. It is inspired by Karl Weick's (1969, 1979, 1995) sensemaking theory, the body of knowledge in MOS that is most closely aligned with the design-as-meaning-making-and-meaning-taking perspective developed by the design community and inspired by the writings of (Krippendorff 1989). Weick has had a fundamental role in the rethinking of the positivist perspective of traditional MOS research (which includes organizational design) and his most influential achievement has been, in our opinion, the breakaway from the rationalist perspective on organization as the outcome of decision-making and the move to organization as the result of continual processes of sensemaking.

Thus, according to the ontological view, organization design is explained as an evolutionary process of meaning, where three types of sensemaking components interact dynamically: (i) the social form, as the basic sensemaking engine operating at the intersubjective level; (ii) the organizational structure, made up of formal and informal components which together make up the realized structure, perpetually swinging back and forth between improvisation and formalization; (iii) the organization design gestalt as a sensemaking process of cultural construction, where symbolic, ethic and aesthetic meanings combine to generate the holistic "experience of the organization".

Organization Designing

The last part of the book covers the topic of organization designing and aims at explaining how the holistic organization design model works in practice. It develops the three topics that make up the normative component—morality, collaboration and purpose—from the point of view of the *organization designer*, a managerial role which has hitherto not been part of the traditional roles of the manager. It is conceived as a generalist role to be mastered and practised by all managers, although in the case of large organizations it may be set up as a separate role, like finance or marketing. As already mentioned, the role is conceptualized at two levels of intervention: a technical level focusing on effectiveness and efficiency of operations, and a higher level, geared towards an instilling of principles and values derived from the organization's purpose throughout the organizational activity. This is achieved not only through the organization's artefacts, but also through the interactions, relationships and experiences mediated by the artefacts.

Organization designing is complementary of strategic management, in the sense that the designing role is also required to assess and evaluate organizational performance but using a new type of yardstick—sensory/aesthetic/experiential—in addition to the regular rational-instrumental measures of peformance. The rational-instrumental capabilities are the usual analytical skills that managers are expected to have, whereas the sensory/aesthetic/experiential capabilities are much harder to pinpoint because they are encapsulated in the person's aesthetic knowledge and depend on the person's aesthetic sensitivity. Crucially, aesthetic sensitivity includes a capacity for reflexivity, as well as the capacity to question oneself, one's feelings, one's motives and one's role in the organization. Aesthetic reflexive practice is one of the key competencies behind responsible management (Cunliffe 2009) as well as the driving force behind morality in the organization (Dobson 2022). Hence, in our model morality is not something that is imposed from the outside of the organization but is a quality that is endogenous, developed internally by the organization's members, starting with the managers.

The book concludes with a call to the MOS community for a rethink of the mindset and the education system, which continues to preserve the traditional organization design paradigm. The proposed meaning-based, sensory and ethic-aesthetic interpretation of organization design provides an opportunity to review positivist organization theory. In conceiving organization designing as something holistic and covering every corner of the organizational realm, a new managerial role with aesthetic and deontological responsibilities, in addition to the traditional performance-related duties, is suggested.

The Methodology

In terms of methodology, the book is based on the narrative-based style of research as one of possible writing styles for theory development in MOS, which is succinctly described by Cornelissen (2017: 3) as "the specification of a process model that lays out a set of mechanisms explaining events and outcomes". The explanatory model at the centre of the book is intended to explain organization design as a meaning-driven process and simultaneously provide an analytical basis for further development. Moreover, the book heeds the advice from Kilduff (2006) and Corley and Gioia (2011) about the need to develop theory in MOS that is prescient (i.e., anticipating future research directions) and that contributes to reducing the gap between theory and practice. Kilduff notes that good theory building in MOS should be guided not by gaps in the literature but by an "engagement with problems in the world" (ibid.: 252), while Corley and Gioia make a strong case for theory that is useful rather than theory that is (scientifically) true. These authors remind us that we belong to a scholarly field that is intimately associated with a domain of *professional practice*, a point that is very pertinent to organization design research and the way it has become disconnected from the world of practice.

Thus, by highlighting the "disanalogy" (Oswick et al. 2011) on which the current understanding of organization design is based (i.e., "design" as in organization design vs. "design" as per the design discipline) and by seeking to refocus the conversation on issues of ethics and aesthetics, our methodological approach seeks to reconnect organization design with real-life societal issues. We also argue that, rather than being approached from a unidirectional perspective (i.e., contingency theory), organization design requires a multidisciplinary perspective, blending design with several key themes from MOS, such as sensemaking and the sub-disciplines of organizational ethics and aesthetics.

The Line-Up

The book opens with Part I, discussing the need to bring meaning, values and behaviour to organization design thinking, and it features two chapters: Chapter 2, covering the topics of situated organization design, and the design discipline; and Chapter 3, focused on non-representational thought, ethics and aesthetics. In Part II, the new approach is introduced, with a brief chapter on organizational artefacts, followed by a more substantial Chapter 5 discussing the reasons why organization design should not be seen as a unitary construct. In Chapter 6, the holistic organization design model starts to be described, with a discussion about morality, collaboration and purpose as the normative imperatives. This is followed by an argument about non-representational thought as the epistemological backdrop. Chapters 7 and 8 are dedicated to the hypothesis of organization design as meaning, firstly with an explanation about how organization design can be conceived as sensemaking and structuration, and next with a description of the concept of organization design gestalt. Part III is about organization designing and contains two chapters: Chapter 9, covering the topics of coordination as an aestho-instrumental organizational capability and the ethic-aesthetic vision; and Chapter 10, on the topic of organizational morality, through aesthetic leadership, reflective practice and responsible management. The final chapter ends with a brief discussion about the need for us—management educators and researchers—to transform ourselves to transform societies. The book ends with a Conclusion, where the book's main topics are brought together and synthesized.

References

Ackoff, R.L. 1981. *Creating the Future*. New York: Wiley.

Amis, J., S. Brickson, P. Haack, and M. Hernandez. 2021. Taking Inequality Seriously. *Academy of Management Review* 46 (3): 431–439.

Avital, M., and D. Te'eni. 2009. From Generative Fit to Generative Capacity: Exploring an Emerging Dimension of Information Systems Design and Task Performance. *Information Systems Journal* 19: 345–367.

Avital, M., K. Kalle Lyytinen, R.J. Boland, B. Butler, D. Dougherty, M. Fineout, W. Jansen, N. Levina, W. Rifkin, and J. Venable. 2006. Design with a Positive Lens: An Affirmative Approach to Designing Information and Organizations. *Communications of the Association for Information Systems* 18: 519–545.

Baldessarelli, G., I. Stigliani, and K.D. Elsbach. 2022. The Aesthetic Dimension of Organizing: A Review and Research Agenda. *Academy of Management Annals* 16: 217–257.

Barnard, C.I. 1938. *The Functions of the Executive*. Cambridge, MA: Harvard University Press.

Barnard, C.I. 1958. Elementary Conditions of Business Morals. *California Management Review* 1 (1): 1–13.

Barry, D. 2011. Re-designing Organization Design. Paper presented at the Design Business Conference, Barcelona, November 17–18.

Bate, P., R. Khan, and A. Pye. 2000. Towards a Culturally Sensitive Approach to Organizational Structuring: Where organization design meets organization development. *Organization Science* 11 (2): 197–211.

Bernacchio, C., N.J. Foss, and S. Lindenberg. 2022. The Virtues of Joint Production: Ethical Foundations for Collaborative Organization. *Academy of Management Review*, published online: 8 September 2022. https://doi.org/10.5465/amr.2019.0389.

Boland, R.J., and F. Collopy. 2004. *Managing as Designing*. Stanford, CA: Stanford University Press.

Boland, R.J., F. Collopy, K. Lyytinen, and Y. Yoo. 2008. Managing as Designing: Lessons for Organization Leaders from the Design Practice of Frank O. Gehry. *Design Issues* 24 (1): 10–25.

Bonsiepe, G. 2006. Design and Democracy. *Design Issues* 22 (2): 27–34.

Ciborra, C.U. 1996. The Platform Organization: Recombining Strategies, Structures and Surprises. *Organization Science* 7: 103–118.

Clegg, S. 1994. Weber and Foucault: Social Theory for the Study of Organizations. *Organization* 1 (1): 149–178.

Corley, K.G., and D.A. Gioia. 2011. "Building Theory About Theory Building": What Constitutes a Theoretical Contribution? *Academy of Management Review* 36 (1): 12–32.

Cornelissen, J. 2017. Editor's Comments: Developing Propositions, a Process Model, or a Typology? Addressing the Challenges of Writing Theory Without a Boilerplate. *Academy of Management Review* 42 (1): 1–9.

Cunliffe, A.L. 2009. The Philosopher Leader: "On Relationalism, Ethics and Reflexivity—A Critical Perspective to Teaching Leadership. *Management Learning* 40 (1): 87–101.

Dobson, J. 2004. Applying Virtue Ethics to Business: The Agent-Based Approach. *EJBO—Electronic Journal of Business Ethics and Organization Studies, 9*(1). http://ejbo.jyu.fi

Dobson, J. 2007. Aesthetics as a Foundation for Business Activity. *Journal of Business Ethics* 72: 41–46.

Dobson, J. 2010. Aesthetic Style as a Postructural Business Ethic. *Journal of Business Ethics* 93: 393–400.

Dobson, J. 2022. Virtue Ethics, Aesthetics, and Reflective Practices in Business. *Philosophy of Management* 21: 493–505.

Donaldson, T., and L.E. Preston. 1995. The Stakeholder Theory of the Corporation: Concepts, Evidence, and Implications. *Academy of Management Review* 20 (1): 43–65.

Dunbar, R.L.M., A.G.L. Romme, and W.H. Starbuck. 2008. Creating Better Understanding of Organizations While Building Better Organizations. In *Sage Handbook of New Approaches in Management and Organization*, ed. D. Barry and H. Hansen. London: Sage.

Freeman, R.E. 1984. *Strategic Management: A Stakeholder Approach*. Boston: Pitman.

Garud, R., A. Kumaraswamy, and V. Sambamurthy. 2006. Emergent by Design: Performance and Transformation at Infosys Technologies. *Organization Science* 17: 277–286.

Garud, R., S. Jain, and P. Tuertscher. 2008. Incomplete by Design and Designing for Incompleteness. *Organization Studies* 29: 351–371.

George, G., M.R. Haas, A.M. McGahan, S.J.D. Schillebeeckx, and P. Tracey. 2023. Purpose in the For-Profit Firm: A Review and Framework for Management Research. *Journal of Management* 49 (6): 1841–1869.

Ghoshal, S. 2005. Bad Management Theories Are Destroying Good Management Practices. *Academy of Management Learning & Education* 4: 75–91.

Harrison, J.S., J.B. Barney, R.E. Freeman, and R.A. Phillips, eds. 2019. *The Cambridge Handbook of Stakeholder Theory*. Cambridge: Cambridge University Press.

Jelinek, M., A.G.L. Romme, and R.J. Boland. 2008. Introduction to the Special Issue Organization Studies as a Science for Design: Creating Collaborative Artifacts and Research. *Organization Studies* 29 (3): 317–329.

Kilduff, M. 2006. Editor's Comments: Publishing Theory. *Academy of Management Review* 31: 252–255.

Kimberly, J.R. 1984. The Anatomy of Organizational Design. *Journal of Management* 10 (1): 109–126.

Krippendorff, K. 1989. On the Essential Contexts of Artifacts or on the Proposition That "Design Is Making Sense of Things". *Design Issues* 5: 9–39.

Krippendorff, K. 2006. The Semantic Turn: a new foundation for design. *Boca Raton*, FL: Taylor and Francis

MacIntyre, A. 2007. *After Virtue*, 3rd ed. London: Duckworth.

Manzini, E. 2015. *Design When Everybody Designs. An Introduction to Design for Social Innovation*. Cambridge: MIT Press.

McEvily, B., G. Soda, and M. Tortoriello. 2014. More Formally: Rediscovering the Missing Link Between Formal Organization and Informal Social Structure. *Academy of Management Annals* 8 (1): 299–345.

Nonaka, I., and H. Takeuchi. 2021. Humanizing Strategy. *Long Range Planning* 54 (4): 102070.

Oswick, C., P. Fleming, and G. Hanlon. 2011. From Borrowing to Blending: Rethinking the Processes of Organizational Theory Building. *Academy of Management Review* 36: 318–337.

Parrish, B.D. 2010. Sustainability-Driven Entrepreneurship: Principles of Organization Design. *Journal of Business Venturing* 25: 510–523.

Pye, A. 1994. Walking and Talking Chester I. Barnard. *International Journal of Public Administration* 17 (6): 1125–1156.

Reckwitz, A. 2012. Affective Spaces: A Praxeological Outlook. *Rethinking History* 16 (2): 241–258.

Rindova, V.P., and S. Kotha. 2001. Continuous "Morphing": Competing Through Dynamic Capabilities, Form, and Function. *Academy of Management Journal* 44: 1263–1280.

Romme, A.G.L., and G. Endenburg. 2006. Construction Principles and Design Rules in the Case of Circular Design. *Organization Science* 17: 287–297.

Sarasvathy, S., N. Dew, S. Read, and R. Wiltbank. 2008. Designing Organizations That Design Environments: Lessons from Entrepreneurial Expertise. *Organization Studies* 29: 331–350.

Shrivastava, P., G. Schumacher, D.M. Wasieleski, and M. Tasic. 2017. Aesthetic Rationality in Organizations: Toward Developing a Sensitivity for Sustainability. *The Journal of Applied Behavioural Science* 53 (3): 369–411.

Simon, H. A. 1996. The Sciences of the Artificial, 3rd edition. Cambridge, MA: MIT Press

Snow, C.C., and O.D. Fjeldstat, eds. 2024. *Designing Adaptive Organizations*. Cambridge: Cambridge University Press.

Taylor, S.S., and H. Hansen. 2005. Finding Form: Looking at the Field of Organizational Aesthetics. *Journal of Management Studies* 42 (6): 1211–1231.

Thrift, N. 2008. *Non-Representational Theory: Space, Politics, Affect*. London: Routledge.

van Aken, J.E. 2004. Management Research Based on the Paradigm of the Design Sciences: The Quest for Field-Tested and Grounded Technological Rules. *Journal of Management Studies* 41 (2): 119–246.

van Aken, J.E., and G. Romme. 2009. Reinventing the Future: Adding Design Science to the Repertoire of Organization and Management Studies. *Organization Management Journal* 6: 5–12.

Van de Ven, A.H., M. Ganco, and C.B. Hinings. 2014. Returning to the Frontier of Contingency Theory of Organizational and Institutional Designs. *The Academy of Management Annals* 7: 393–440.

Verganti, R. 2009. *Design-Driven Innovation: Changing the Rules of Competition by Radically Innovating What Things Mean*. Boston, MA: Harvard Business Press.

Verganti, R. 2016. *Overcrowded: Designing Meaningful Products in a World Awash with Ideas*. Cambridge, MA: MIT Press.

Weick, K.E. 1969. *The Social Psychology of Organizing*. Reading, MA: Addison-Wesley.

Weick, K.E. 1979. *The Social Psychology of Organizing*, 2nd ed. Reading, MA: Addison-Wesley.

Weick, K.E. 1995. *Sensemaking in Organizations*. Beverly Hills, CA: Sage.

Weick, K.E. 2004. Rethinking Organization Design. In *Managing as Designing*, ed. R.J. Boland and F. Collopy. Stanford, CA: Stanford University Press.

Yoo, Y., Boland, R., and Lytinen, K. 2006. From Organization Design to Organization Designing. *Organization Science*, 17: 215–229

Zammuto, R.F., T.L. Griffith, A. Majchrzak, D.J. Dougherty, and S. Faraj. 2007. Information Technology and the Changing Fabric of Organization. *Organization Science* 18 (5): 749–762.

PART I

About the Need to Bring Meaning, Values and Behaviour to Organization Design Thinking

The evolution of organization design thinking has been outlined and described by many writers and for this reason the exercise will not be repeated here. In a nutshell, this field has been dominated by the contingency approach, according to which the most effective structural arrangements for the organization happen when the structure fits the environmental contingencies (Donaldson 2006). The intellectual stance underpinning the contingency approach is positivist in nature, meaning that the final aim would be to establish testable theories about the structural configurations which would enhance the organization's chances of maximizing its performance (Clegg et al. 2005).

Notably, what all the trends derived from or related to contingency theory have in common is the fact that none acknowledge people as an element in the study of organization design. Organization designs are "things" whose operation can be manipulated by predetermined rules. Over the years, there have been many voices against this, one of the earliest being that of Goulder (1954) and his well-known study on the patterns of industrial bureaucracy, where the key finding was that more than rules and procedures, bureaucracy is about people (Hallett & Ventresca, 2006) . In traditional organization theory, very few writers have dared go against the contingency orthodoxy, the notable exception being Weick (2001) with the suggestion that organization design is all about improvisation. Building on that scholar's ideas, and on the research on improvisation that has followed, the notion of organizational form/

design shifts from something monolithic and imposed from the outside, to a more endogenous, generative, socially constructed, holistic, virtual and circular view of the organization, not directly dependent upon environmental forces, but with the in-built capacity to initiate changes in the environment (Boland et al. 2008; Dunbar et al. 2008; Garud et al. 2006; Garud et al. 2008; Romme 1999; Romme and Endenburg 2006; Sarasvathy et al. 2008). We call this position *situated organization design*.

But organization design can also be viewed from the point of view of its product, i.e., the organization, and here we sense that there is a persistent feeling that organizations of all types are somehow not contributing towards the welfare of society. Buchanan (2015) suggests that the widespread dissatisfaction with the role of organization might be traced to a variety of *design flaws*. For management scholars, the causes for organizational problems are financial, technological, strategic and perhaps behavioural, but they are never perceived as "design problems". The reason for this is the enduring *chasm* between the world of management and design as a discipline.

Broadly speaking, design can be defined as the activities of "giving real existence—form, structure and shape—to [an] idea" (Nelson and Stolterman 2014: 1). However, not all designs are the same. Nelson and Stolterman explain that if the designer's intention is to create artefacts that will have a long-lasting effect and designs that will "extend, augment and ennoble" (Ibid, p. 192) the designer's achievements, then functionality or efficiency is insufficient as the applicable measures. (...) They state:

> Sometimes design becomes a conveyor of soul (...) Quality is not robust enough as a scale of measurement against which to judge "good" design. At least, this holds if the ambition is to create designs that have a positive and lasting impact on our reality (Ibid, p. 192).

These authors suggest that traditional measurements, such as quality are not applicable to certain types of design, and that the meanings embedded in those designs must be valued and judged by their intrinsic value or by the experiences they evoke. Given that organizations are usually set with ambitious long-term aims that go beyond purely instrumental motives, organizational design fits well with this type of approach. More than other types of design, organizations can also be said to have a "soul", that is, they have values and, as Nelson and Stolterman suggest, functionality, efficiency, effectiveness or competitiveness is not sufficient as qualities to assess the design of an organization.

Consequently, we submit that design theory should be explored as an appropriate source of inspiration for organization design research, but given that design itself has different epistemological influences, the question of epistemology is still open. In other words, if organization design is to cease following a positivist approach, what would be an appropriate epistemology? Kimbell (2012) proposes the notions of "design-as-practice" and "designing-as-practicing", as an approach to the design discipline that moves away from the instrumental and disembodied perspectives on design thinking to a situated set of practices, which recognize the involvement of stakeholders and the materiality of designed artefacts. Following up this rationale, and in recognition of the need to bring situatedness, meaning, values and behaviour to the study of organization design, Magalhaes (2020) has suggested that design-as-practice and designing-as-practising can readily be applied to a conceptualization of organization design.

The practice approach is sociomaterial, a perspective that grants equal status to the humans and the "more-than-humans" linked within a practice (Gherardi 2016). Sociomateriality and the practice approach are part of a broader school of thought known as non-representational theory, the epistemological approach that we follow in this book, and which we explore in Chapter 2. Chapter 1 is devoted to the topics of situated organization design and the relationship between organization design and design. These two chapters cover the theoretical background that has inspired the writing of this book.

References

Boland, R.J., F. Collopy, K. Lyytinen, and Y. Yoo. 2008. Managing as Designing: Lessons for Organization Leaders from the Design Practice of Frank O. Gehry. *Design Issues* 24 (1): 10–25.

Buchanan, R. 2015. Worlds in the Making: Design, Management, and the Reform of Organizational Culture. *She Ji: The Journal of Design, Economics and Innovation,* 1 (1): 5–21

Clegg, S., M. Kornberg, and T. Pitsis. 2005. *Managing and Organizations. An Introduction to Theory and Practice*. London: Sage.

Donaldson, L. 2006. The Contingency Approach of Organization Design: Challenges and Opportunities. In *Organization Design: The Evolving State-of-the-Art*, ed. R.M. Burton, B. Eriksen, D.D. Hakonsson, and C.C. Snow. New York: Springer.

Dunbar, R. L. M., A.G.L. Romme, and W.H. Starbuck. 2008. Creating Better Understanding of Organizations While Building Better Organizations. In *Sage Handbook of New Approaches in Management and Organization*, ed. D. Barry and H. Hansen. London: Sage.

Garud, R., A. Kumaraswamy, and V. Sambamurthy. 2006. Emergent by Design: Performance and Transformation at Infosys Technologies. *Organization Science* 17: 277–286.

Garud, R., S. Jain, and P. Tuertscher. 2008. Incomplete by Design and Designing for Incompleteness. *Organization Studies* 29: 351–371.

Gherardi, S. 2016. To Start Practice Theorizing Anew: The Contribution of the Concepts of *Agencement* and Formativeness. *Organization* 23 (5): 680–698.

Gouldner, A.W. 1954. *Patterns of Industrial Bureaucracy*. Glencoe, IL: Free Press.

Hallett, T. & Ventresca, M. J. 2006. Inhabited Institutions: social interactions and organizational forms in Gouldner's 'patterns of industrial bureaucracy'. *Theory and Society*, 35 (2): 213–236

Kimbell, L. 2012. Rethinking Design Thinking: Part 2. *Design and Culture* 4 (2): 129–148.

Magalhaes, R. 2020. *Designing Organization Design: A Human-Centred Approach*. Oxford: Oxford University Press.

Nelson, H.G., and E. Stolterman. 2014. *The Design Way: Intentional Change in an Unpredictable World*. Cambridge, MA: MIT Press.

Romme, A.G.L. 1999. Domination, Self-Determination and Circular Organizing. *Organization Studies* 20 (5): 801–831.

Romme, A.G.L., and G. Endenburg. 2006. Construction Principles and Design Rules in the Case of Circular Design. *Organization Science* 17: 287–297.

Sarasvathy, S., N. Dew, S. Read, and R. Wiltbank. 2008. Designing Organizations That Design Environments: Lessons from Entrepreneurial Expertise. *Organization Studies* 29: 331–350.

Weick, K.E. 2001. *Making Sense of the Organization*. Malden, MA: Blackwell.

CHAPTER 2

Organization Design and the Design Discipline

Abstract This chapter covers with broad brushstrokes the background in two fields of knowledge: organization design and design theory as applicable to organization design. In a nutshell, the field of organization design has been dominated by the contingency approach, a trend that treats organization design as being nothing more than structure and division of labour, with people not considered as part of the problem. Organization designs are "things" whose operation can be manipulated by predetermined rules. Over the years, there have been many voices against this, the most notable being that of Karl Weick, with the suggestion that organization design is all about improvisation. Building on that scholar's ideas, the notion of organizational form/design shifts from something monolithic and imposed from the outside, to a more endogenous, generative, socially constructed, holistic, virtual and circular view of the organization, not directly dependent upon environmental forces, but with an in-built capacity to initiate changes in the environment. The second part of the chapter explores key writings in design theory, with a focus on human-centred design, as a school of thought that opposes design as problem-solving, a trend originally launched by the writings of Simon (The Sciences of the Artificial. MIT Press, Cambridge, MA, 1996). Human-centred design, strongly influenced by the writings of Krippendorff (The Semantic Turn: A New Foundation for Design. Taylor and Francis, Boca Raton, FL, 2006), defines design as the creation of meaning and places humanism and ethics at the centre of its concerns.

R. Magalhães, *Designing Organizations for the Betterment of Society*,
https://doi.org/10.1007/978-3-031-64483-2_2

Keywords Aesthetics · Ethics · Design theory · Contingency · Design thinking · Holistic · Human-centred · Krippendorff · Humanism · Meaning · Organization design · Simon · Socially constructed · Virtual · Weick

Situated Organization Design

In the traditional approach, organization designing was seen as an exercise in organizational structuring, with the objective of achieving the best possible structure through the division of the organization's labour into the number of required tasks. However, such division of labour raises coordination issues and coordination mechanisms need to be put in place, so that all the tasks contribute towards the achievement of the organization's mission. Mintzberg (1980) lists nine mechanisms or levers which organizations can use to design their structures—job specialization, behaviour formalization, training and indoctrination, unit grouping, unit size, planning and control systems, liaison devices, vertical decentralization and horizontal decentralization. These levers are intertwined and interdependent, but if there is one that could be called pivotal it would be *behaviour formalization*, the design parameter which allows a distinction between hierarchical or bureaucratic structures and organic ones (Burns and Stalker 1961). Formalization tells us the degree to which work processes are standardized, through rules, procedures, policy manuals, job descriptions, automated and non-automated work systems and so on.

Given the reductionist logic instilled for decades by the contingency paradigm, the received wisdom is that all behaviour in organizations is formalized or formalizable. However, since the publication of Weick's (1969) *Social Psychology of Organizing*, and the suggestion that organizational processes unfold in ways that mirror evolution and natural selection, perceptions of behaviour in organizations began to change. Indeed, Weick (1977) put forward that organizations are self-designing systems and that behaviour in organizations is partly improvised. Based on his work on sensemaking, and on the notion that *sensemaking precedes decision-making*, Weick (2001) discusses a new vision of organization design as improvisation. Table 2.1 shows how the old and the new conceptions of organization design are almost diametrically opposed and how the vision of organization design as improvisation can lead towards a whole new paradigm.

The perspective on organization design as improvisation is supported by the work of several authors. For example, the notions that design is "continuously reconstructed" and that an organization has "multiple designs" are replicated in Rindova and Kotha's (2001) suggestion of organizational form as a process of "continuous morphing", in Yoo et al.'s (2006: 228) conclusion that "organization design becomes a continuous shaping of the organization" and in Romme and Endenburg's (2006) proposal of circular organization, presenting organization design as a continuous loop of planned decisions which need to be permanently adjusted and adapted to the emergent micro-designs at the local level. However, Weick does not develop a new theory of organization design,

Table 2.1 Implied assumptions in a comparison between organization design as structure and organization design as improvisation

Organization design as structure	*Organization design as improvisation*
1. Design is a blueprint	1a. Design is recipe
2. Design is constructed at a single point in time	2a. Design is continuously reconstructed
3. Design produces order through intention	3a. Design produces order through attention
4. Design creates planned change	4a. Design codifies unplanned change after the fact
5. An organization has only a single design	5a. An organization has multiple designs
6. The design determines the distribution of resources	6a. The distribution of resources determines the design
7. Designs are large structures that are stabilized	7a. Designs are smalls structures that are amplified
8. Design affects managerial ability	8a. Managerial ability affects design
9. Managerial action is individual	9a. Managerial action is social
10. [Design-related] decisions determine effectiveness	10a. [Design-related] interpretations determine effectiveness
11. The purpose of design is to facilitate decision making	11a. The purpose of design is to facilitate interpretation
12. People decide [i.e., design] and then they act	12a. People act [i.e., design] and then they interpret

Source Adapted from Weick (2001)

but he does leave many pointers, which can be used to shape new theoretical paths. For example, in saying that the purpose of design is to "facilitate interpretation" and that effectiveness is determined by "interpretations" and not by "decisions" Weick highlights the relevance of meaning in discussions about design.

Theoretical hints for a new approach to organization design can also be derived from the well-established research on organizational improvisation, a phenomenon that Cunha et al. (2016) describe as follows : (i) improvisation is characterized by the "convergence of *design* and performance"; (ii) improvisation involves the creation of some degree of novel action; (iii) improvisation implies the "deliberateness of the *design* that is created as the improvisation is enacted"; (iv) improvisation is referent, meaning that often the improvisation process "involves a prior version of an action pattern or prior plan" (ibid.: 559). Such characterization implies that improvisation represents a special type of unplanned action, which excludes random change and therefore implies a new conception of *(emergent) organizational design*. Given that improvisation is part of the largely "trivial and mundane process of organizational learning" (Cunha and Clegg 2019: 239) rather than something unusual or exceptional, the contributions afforded by improvisation to organization design should also be understood as the ongoing changes to daily practices that may eventually become embedded in the organization's formal structure. This process is described by Garud et al. (2008), under the label of "pragmatic [organization] design", as the fusion of two design modes, i.e., the dynamic mode of design(ing) as a process, and the static mode of design as the outcome of the process.

In drawing attention to the emergent and unplanned nature of organizational improvisation, and to the significance of agency, the literature on situated organization design has downplayed the role of sensory or aesthetic knowledge, that is, the knowledge gained directly from our senses. Affects and emotions have great relevance to the processes of improvisation and as explained by philosophers like Levinson (1998) or Shusterman (2009) aesthetic judgements are closely associated with the ethical judgements that we make throughout our daily lives. Hence, in considering organization design as improvisation, ethics and aesthetics should also be on board as elements in the processes of design(ing). This means that beside the rules that guide the design and operation of organizational artefacts (for example, health and safety rules, corporate governance rules, systems and procedural rules, etc.), there should also be serious consideration of the ethical and aesthetic consequences of such artefacts for the stakeholders. Consider, for example, how some artefacts blatantly facilitate less-than-ethical behaviours and deviations from the organization's core values. In addition to more attention at the level of individual artefacts, there must also be renewed awareness of the need to oversee the practices that lie behind much of the organization's design, from an ethical-aesthetic viewpoint. Normative approaches to organizational design have been persistently avoided throughout the history of this field of knowledge (see, for example, Kilmann et al. 1976 or Jelinek et al. 1981). However, the growing number of cases of unethical behaviour on the part of all types of organizations call for a different stance on the part of MOS researchers and for more attention to the trends towards the integration of the disciplines of management and design (Boland and Collopy 2004), and in particular, to the ethical norms of design as a discipline.

Design Trends and Their Application to Organization Design

Considering that over the years organization theory has borrowed not only from the title of the discipline, but also from design concepts like form and structure, we suggest that it is time for design to be acknowledged and for *design principles* to be adopted as guidelines for organization design. While such principles and ideas are by no means foreign to MOS research, they have not been incorporated into organization design theory and practice in any systematic way. Design scholar Richard Buchanan (2016) reminds us that management is a design discipline and that designers and managers are not two separate groups. He claims that the most important design products of the twentieth century are products of management, i.e., "the design of organizations" and that without this design product "no other design discipline could have any impact on society and the lives of human beings" (ibid.: 19).

In these statements, Buchanan throws new light on the design of organizations, placing it at a level seemingly over and above other areas of design. Such superordinate feature of design is also highlighted by Nelson and Stolterman (2014: 192) in affirming that "quality is not robust enough as a scale of measurement against which to judge 'good' design". Hence, if it is agreed that organization design shares with design "the ability to imagine that-which-does-not-yet-exist, to make it appear in concrete form as a new, purposeful addition to the real world" (Nelson and Stolterman 2014: 12), then it can be argued that organization design as an area of study requires a level of discourse with ***normative overtones***, placed over and above the usual measures of organizational efficiency or effectiveness. Thus, in the theorizing of organization design, design principles must be seen as relevant, especially the principle of design ethics (Krippendorff 2006). In order to better understand how ethics fits in the design movement, it is important to mention three of the major trends of the design discipline—design as problem-solving, human-centred design and design thinking.

Design as Problem-Solving

Design is a paradigm of human knowledge and a new field of study introduced by Herbert Simon (1996) as distinct from the natural sciences and the social sciences and focused on everything that might be labelled "artificial". He called it "science of design", a field applicable to professional schools of thought, such as medicine, engineering or management. As the cornerstone of the new theory of design, Simon advocated the solution of "design problems", with the problem taking the form of a combination of values qualifying a set of key variables, which represent the artefact under study in its own environment. This design method amounted to finding a solution to a given set of constraints, sometimes including the maximization of an "objective function". The assumption underlying such a method is that a design problem can be specified with a high degree of completeness prior to the "search for solutions". To many people, this seems far-fetched in social organizations because it is virtually impossible to specify all the intervening variables at the outset. Thus, in spite of the benefits that formal methods offer in specialized contexts (e.g., software development), a growing number of researchers express the view that Simon's idea of a new general "science of design" raises some serious doubts (Galle 2011). As a consequence, alternative approaches have emerged under the growing belief that design problems and design solutions necessarily "co-evolve".

Design as Creation of Meaning

Although very popular among the engineering and management communities, Simon's decision-making model began to be questioned as a method for approaching problems in the real world of people and organizations. One of the reasons behind this turn is the emergence of the notion that design can be seen as a "hermeneutical circle" (Snodgrass and Coyne 1992, 1997), or a process of interpretation conceived as a dialogical exchange between the designer and the design situation. This idea was originally developed by Schon (1983), who suggests that an important skill for managers to develop is reflection-in-action, to be used in interventions such as "on-the-spot surfacing, criticizing, restructuring and testing intuitive understandings of experienced phenomenon" (ibid.: 241). Hence, reflection-in-action might be summed up as a skilled process of trial and error based on cycles of meaning-giving and meaning-taking that organization designers learn in order to make sense of the informal and emergent issues of organizational life.

Such emphasis on the meanings of artefacts has been theorized by Krippendorff (1989, 2006) under the label of ***human-centred design***. He defines design as "making something, distinguishing it by ***a sign***, giving it significance, designating its relation to other things, owners, users or gods" (1989: 10, italics added). In his book *The Semantic Turn*, Krippendorff (2006: 42) states that "construction and design are synonymous", thus aligning human-centred design with the premise from constructionist social theory that reality is made up by the meanings that are negotiated and agreed upon by the participants (Gergen 1985). Hence, in relation to Simon's (1996) teachings, ***human-centred design*** reverses the relation between the design object and its intention. For Simon, the artefact is at the core and design becomes the method for creating or modifying the artefact. However, for the followers of the human-centred trend, meaning is the core of the design process, and the artefact becomes a medium for communicating the meanings intended by the designer and perceived by the user (Johansson-Sköldberg et al. 2013).

Design Ethics

When creating artefacts, designers are not just solving practical problems, but they are also, at every step, affecting people, their well-being and the way they work or live together. When designers devise courses of action aimed at changing existing situations into preferred ones, the resulting artefacts might not necessarily be good for everyone. Krippendorff (2006) argues that design cannot avoid ethical questions, and states:

> it is a matter of ethics to acknowledge multiple stakeholders in design. (Krippendorff 2006: 322)

Moreover, he clarifies that:

> As soon as we move beyond the engineering of functional products, we need to be concerned with what the artefacts of design could possibly *mean* to users and interested parties, with the multiple rationalities that people can bring to bear on them. (Krippendorff 2011: 413)

An example of designing for multiple stakeholders comes from urban planning, where the design solutions found for one group of people might not be suitable for the rest of the community. Therefore, designers must acknowledge and take into account the needs and aspirations of the people who are affected by the design proposals and have a good grasp of which proposals constitute a betterment and which create a problem. Buchanan (2001) emphasizes that "the quality of design is distinguished not merely by technical skill of execution or by aesthetic vision but by the moral and intellectual purpose toward which technical and artistic skill is directed" (ibid.: 37). Bonsiepe (2006), on the other hand, asserts that humanism in the field of design means that designers can play a role in reducing the domination over "the excluded, the discriminated, and economically less-favored groups" (ibid.: 30). Thus, design ethics assumes a degree of accountability on the part of the designer, not only towards the stakeholders of current projects, but also as the moral agent seeking *ethical ways of building the future* (Buchanan 2022).

Thus, human-centred design has initiated a turn in the design discipline away from the rationality of decision-making and in the direction of design as human meanings, feelings and sensitivities. This turn is also noticeable in the so-called design thinking movement, where although the initial emphasis was on something done "for" the organization, in more recent academic literature it begins to emerge as something that should be inherent "in" the organization.

The Aesthetics of Design Thinking

In the last couple of decades, design thinking has become a popular trend in business management literature as a set of methods aimed at introducing innovation-prone management styles, and although the focus has not been on the organization-wide implications of design, some authors have begun to recognize the need for design thinking to embrace broader issues such as organizational design or aesthetics. Micheli et al. (2019: 22) assert that "organizational design is a necessary condition for successful design thinking", while Elsbach and Stigliani (2018) suggest that the use of design thinking tools and techniques produces emotional and material experiences that improve our understanding of collaboration, sensemaking and empathy in organizations. In addition, these authors put forward that design thinking enables a kind of *experiential learning*, which can also be seen against a background of organizational aesthetics. Indeed, design thinking touches on a number of topics that have a clear aesthetic reading, such as the visual approach, thinking by doing, holistic view, or integrative thinking.

Design thinking studies oriented towards marketing and customer services have explicitly highlighted aesthetics as a key feature of a new conception of customer value associated with form, appearance, experience and the feel of design (Tonkinwise 2011). Venkatesh et al. (2012) talk of an emerging *aesthetic imperative* to signify the way in which design has come to represent a novel mode of creating customer value. Such evolution considers design as a factor that enhances products and services, not only in terms of surface aesthetic qualities but in terms of deeper sensory content. In brief, design thinking is an important trend, not only due to the argument that design techniques have business value that can (and should) be applied to regular operational management, but also due to the suggestion that design thinking enables a kind of *experiential learning* (Elsbach and Stigliani 2018). Design thinking can thus become a tool for fostering a *culture of (organization) design*, associated with the aesthetics of organizational experience, and consequently with the ethics associated with aesthetic sensibility and aesthetic judgement.

References

Boland, R.J., and F. Collopy. 2004. *Managing as Designing*. Stanford, CA: Stanford University Press.

Bonsiepe, G. 2006. Design and Democracy. *Design Issues* 22 (2): 27–34.

Buchanan, R. 2001. Human Dignity and Human Rights: Thoughts on the Principles of Human-Centred Design. *Design Issues* 17 (3): 35–39.

Buchanan, R. 2016. Design on New Ground: The Turn to Action, Services and Management. In *Designing Business and Management*, ed. S. Junginger and J. Faust. London: Bloomsbury Academic.

Buchanan, R. 2022. *Design Ethics*. Encyclopedia.com. Retrieved on 20 August 2022 from https://www.encyclopedia.com/science/encyclopedias-almanacs-transcripts-and-maps/design-ethics.

Burns, T. & Stalker, G. 1961. *The Management of Innovation*. London: Tavistock Publications

Cunha, M.P., and C. Clegg. 2019. Improvisation in the Learning Organization: A Defense of the Infra-Ordinary. *The Learning Organization* 26 (3): 238–251.

Cunha, M.P., A.S. Miner, and E. Antonacopolou. 2016. Improvisation Processes in Organizations. In *The Sage Handbook of Process Organization Studies*, ed, A. Langley and H. Tsoukas. Los Angeles, CA: Sage.

Elsbach, K.D., and I. Stigliani. 2018. Design Thinking and Organizational Culture: A Review and Framework for Future Research. *Journal of Management* 44 (6): 1–33.

Galle, P. 2011. Foundational and Instrumental Design Theory. *Design Issues*, 27 (4): 81–94

Garud, R., S. Jain, and P. Tuertscher. 2008. Incomplete by Design and Designing for Incompleteness. *Organization Studies* 29: 351–371.

Gergen, K.J. 1985. The Social Constructionist Movement in Modern Psychology. *American Psychologist* 40 (3): 266–275.

Jelinek, M., J.A. Litterer, and R.E. Miles, eds. 1981. *Organizations by Design: Theory and Practice*. Plano, TX: Business Publications.

Johansson-Sköldberg, U., J. Woodilla, and M. Çetinkaya. 2013. Design Thinking: Past, Present and Possible Futures. *Creativity and Innovation Management* 22: 121–146.

Kilmann, R.H., L.R. Pondy, and D.P. Slevin, eds. 1976. *The Management of Organization Design: Research and Methodology*. New York: North-Holland.

Krippendorff, K. 1989. On the Essential Contexts of Artifacts or on the Proposition That "Design Is Making Sense of Things". *Design Issues* 5: 9–39.

Krippendorff, K. 2006. *The Semantic Turn: A New Foundation for Design*. Boca Raton, FL: Taylor and Francis.

Krippendorff, K. 2011. Principles of Design and a Trajectory of Artificiality. *Journal of Production and Innovation Management* 28: 411–418.

Levinson, J. 1998. Aesthetics and Ethics. In *Aesthetics and Ethics: Essays at the Intersection*, ed. J. Levinson. Cambridge: Cambridge University Press.

Micheli. P., Wilner, S. J. S., Bhatti, S. H., Mura, M & Beverland, M. B. 2019. Doing Design Thinking: conceptual review, synthesis, and research agenda. *Journal of Product Innovation Management*, 36 (2): 124–148

Mintzberg, H. 1980. Structure in 5's: A Synthesis of the Research on Organization Design. *Management Science* 26 (3): 322–341.
Nelson, H.G., and E. Stolterman. 2014. *The Design Way: Intentional Change in an Unpredictable World*. Cambridge, MA: MIT Press.
Rindova, V.P., and S. Kotha. 2001. Continuous 'Morphing': Competing Through Dynamic Capabilities, Form, and Function. *Academy of Management Journal* 44: 1263–1280.
Romme, A.G.L., and G. Endenburg. 2006. Construction Principles and Design Rules in the Case of Circular Design. *Organization Science* 17: 287–297.
Schon, D.A. 1983. *The Reflective Practitioner: How Professionals Think in Action*. New York: Basic Books.
Shusterman, R.M. 2009. The Convergence of Ethics and Aesthetics: A Genealogical, Pragmatist Perspective. In *The Hand and the Soul: Ethics and Aesthetics in Architecture and Art*, ed. S. Iliescu. Charlottesville, VA: University of Virginia Press.
Simon, H.A. 1996. *The Sciences of the Artificial*, 3rd ed. Cambridge, MA: MIT Press.
Snodgrass, A., and R. Coyne. 1992. Models, Metaphors and the Hermeneutics of Designing. *Design Issues* 9 (1): 56–74.
Snodgrass, A., and R. Coyne. 1997. Is Designing Hermeneutical? *Architectural Theory Review* 2 (1): 65–97.
Tonkinwise, C. 2011. A Taste for Practices: Unrepressing Style in Design Thinking. *Design Studies* 32 (6): 533–554.
Venkatesh, A., T. Digerfeldt-Mansson, F.F. Brunel, and S. Chen. 2012. Design Orientation: A Grounded Theory Analysis of Design Thinking and Action. *Marketing Theory* 12 (3): 289–309
Weick, K.E. 1969. *The Social Psychology of Organizing*. Reading, MA: Addison-Wesley.
Weick, K.E. 1977. Organization Design: Organizations as Self-Designing Systems. *Organizational Dynamics* 6 (2): 31–46.
Weick, K.E. 2001. *Making Sense of the Organization*. Malden, MA: Blackwell.
Yoo, Y., R. Boland, and K. Lytinen. 2006. From Organization Design to Organization Designing. *Organization Science* 17: 215–229.

CHAPTER 3

Non-representational Thought, Ethics and Aesthetics

Abstract The chapter tackles non-representational thought, briefly explained as an attempt to capture the onflow of organizational life. This approach allows organization design to free itself from the representational notion of organization design-as-structure and opens up the possibility of theorizing organization design as action (i.e., designing). Non-representational thought utilizes several epistemological tools, the main one being practice theory, a sociomaterial approach that grants equal status to the humans and the "more-than-humans". This is relevant to organization design, in so far as organization design also deals with human and non-human actors. The other epistemological tool utilized by non-representational thought is aesthetics as a material, embodied and pre-cognitive component of human knowledge, an element of organizational life now widely recognized by MOS. Aesthetic elements of organizational life originate from "felt meanings", as well as from judgements that people make based on their sensory experience. These are value judgements that enable people to judge "beauty", "taste" or "melodious", but at the same time they also people to judge what is "fair", "just" or "ethical". In this way, aesthetics provides new relevance and visibility to organizational ethics through the relationship between aesthetic rationality and the ethical values that ought to steer organization design.

Keywords Aesthetics · Embodied · Epistemology · Ethics · Material · Non-representational · Pre-cognitive · Sensory

R. Magalhães, *Designing Organizations for the Betterment of Society*,
https://doi.org/10.1007/978-3-031-64483-2_3

Non-representational theory is a body of knowledge emerging from the field of human geography that can be briefly explained as an attempt to capture the onflow of everyday life. It derives from the work of Bourdieu (1990), the author who coined the expression "logic of practice", in opposition to a world view of "intellectualocentrism" (ibid.: 29), a stance that imposes an academic logic of causality, intentionality or instrumentality on practical issues of life and behaviour. Non-representational approaches concentrate on practices, which are defined as "material bodies of work or styles that have gained enough stability over time, through for example, the establishment of corporeal routines and specialized devices" (Thrift 2008: 8). Having said this, it is important to point out that practices are not inherently stable, but instead they are permanently enacted, "producing a continually changing distribution of intensities" (Thrift 2000, cited by Beyes and Steyaert 2012: 52). Additionally, practices are sociomaterial, with Gherardi (2016: 693) explaining that instead of thinking in terms of "actors and their practices", a sociomaterial perspective views the practice as the unit of analysis, defined as an ecology in which all the practice elements are connected.

Reckwitz (2012) argues that every social practice denotes a specific use of the senses and of their perceptive qualities, therefore it can be argued that each practice shapes sensations and perceptions in specific ways. Affects, senses and perceptions are closely interconnected and the idea of being actively affected by something, or someone always suggests a two-way outcome. In other words, in establishing a connection between a body and other objects or other bodies which are perceived and sensed, one has to allow for the possibility that the parties involved are predisposed not only "to be affect" but also "to affect". For Reckwitz, the materiality of practices is anchored not only in bodies, but also in artefacts. For example, a safety belt is not just a neutral non-human object; depending on the situation where/when it is being used, a safety belt can be a bearer of positive or negative affects and can be considered a social actor in its relationship with its user. Hence, from a practice theory perspective, artefacts can be generators of affects, which in turn means that practices are also intrinsically affective (Reckwitz 2017).

Also, practice entails habituation, as explained by Tsoukas (2018):

> habituation involves agents developing both a *moral* sensibility and an *affective* orientation, which enables agents to relate spontaneously to situations. People learn what matters through practice and, as a result, approach

> practical matters affectively. Since emotions disclose to people what matters to them in a situation, they constitute forms of evaluative judgment concerning what is important and how it ought to be responded to. (ibid.: 329, original citations omitted)

Hence, the affective component of social practices has another important implication. It draws the discussion to the realm of aesthetics and aesthetic judgements. Gorodeisky and Marcus (2018) explain that aesthetic judgement is a "sensory-affective disclosure of merit" (ibid.: 113), and by merit they mean a feeling that presents and is responsive to an object that is worthy of being liked. Thus, an aesthetic judgement an be explained as a positive affective attitude towards the object, or a distinctive form of liking, also known as appreciation. Unlike blind sensation, aesthetic liking has a cognitive capability insofar as it constitutes an experience in which the world reveals itself to us; like other perceptions, aesthetic liking has the power to reveal the world immediately rather than mediately. In more conventional language, aesthetics is about "the thinking of the body". It is about the sensory world in which "individuals are immersed since birth, and by virtue of which they act and interact in both their everyday work and private lives" (Strati 2015: 256).

Ethics and Aesthetics

Over the last three decades, the field of organizational aesthetics has been growing in relevance for MOS, but the publication of the major review of the literature by Baldessarelli et al. (2022) published in the Academy of Management Annals can be said to mark the *maturity stage* of the field. The authors acknowledge that the aesthetic dimension of organizing changes our perspective of behaviour in organizations by shedding new light on the role of materiality and related sensory mechanisms on individual- and organization-level processes. Organizational aesthetics has emerged as a sub-discipline of management that invites scholars and practitioners to pay attention to non-rational elements of organizational life and to engender an alternative perspective on many of the taken-for-granted precepts from mainstream organization and management studies. Aesthetic elements of organizational life originate from perceptions or "felt meanings", as well as from judgements that people make, based especially on their sensory experience (Warren 2008). Indeed, aesthetics offers "alternative ways of expressing and making meanings that deeply influence organizational interactions, behaviours, and understandings" (Taylor and Hansen 2005: 1227).

Strati (2015) puts forward some compelling arguments as to why organizational aesthetics should be taken seriously. Although not doing full justice to the depth of Strati's claims, the following points provide a foretaste:

i. Most relevant of all, aesthetics is a pervasive phenomenon in society at large and in organizations in particular; the workplaces, the rhythms of the work, the technologies in use, the relationships among members, the managerial strategies and many organizational decisions not only result from aesthetic choices but also elicit a range of aesthetic feelings.
ii. The study of aesthetics in organizations highlights how organizations are experienced aesthetically beyond their visual and physical appearance; the materiality of organizational life gives salience to the experiential and situated nature of the organization, emphasizing the organization as a "down-to-earth sensible experience rather than an objective reality that transcends the intersubjectivities of the people who inhabit it" (Strati 2015: 253).
iii. Sensible knowledge concerns what is perceived and judged through the senses and is closely related to the emotions of organizational actors; it represents the outcome of what is emotionally or affectively connected with what is perceived.
iv. Aesthetics provides new relevance and visibility to organizational ethics through the relationship between aesthetic rationality and the ethical values that ought to steer organizational life.

Indeed, the study of aesthetics provides new relevance to the issue of organizational ethics, especially if we focus on the relationship between aesthetic rationality and ethical values. The philosopher Richard Shusterman (2009) is among those who argue against treating ethics and aesthetics as separate fields of knowledge, claiming that the chasm between the two is the result of socio-political strains in the development of Western modernity. He argues that a strict division between the two fields of knowledge does not match the reality of human values or experience and explains that ethics and aesthetics are, indeed, convergent. This can be confirmed by our regular use of everyday vocabulary. For example, our moral values lead us to speak of things being "right", "just", "fair" or "appropriate", but when reflecting upon it, it is evident that all such terms have aesthetic connotations and can also be used to signify aesthetic qualities, such as "balance", "order" or "beauty". He states:

> We typically experience the value of noble deeds and exemplary artworks first as a unified whole of value without distinguishing, as separate or opposed, the ethical and aesthetic dimensions of this excellence. In our appreciation of a Shakespearean tragedy or a Henry James novel, we do not first appreciate their artistic skill and moral intelligence as separate factors and then combine them. We instead experience an exquisitely unified synthesis where the ethical and the aesthetic *vision* are so interlaced that one can only subsequently distinguish them by refined intellectual abstraction. (Shusterman 2004: 21, italics added)

Such close intertwining between ethical and aesthetic judgements is also highlighted by Ladkin (2018). Citing the philosopher Jerrold Levinson (1998), Ladkin put forward that the connection between aesthetics and ethics is based on the notion of aesthetics as a way of knowing, and on the realization that both are branches of value theory. In other words, both ethics and aesthetics require knowledge aimed at focusing our sense-making on particular aspects of the environment, as well as enabling judgements about actions or desired affects. Aesthetic knowledge allows one to make judgements about quality and affect, whereas in the realm of ethics judgements are made between right and wrong, and about the most appropriate way to handle various forms of relationships—interpersonal, stakeholder-related or broader social issues.

To understand the link between ethics and aesthetics, it is also important to say something about aesthetic rationality. Gorodeisky and Marcus (2018) argue that the aesthetic domain falls inside the scope of rationality and that the aim of aesthetic judgement is neither belief nor intention, but appreciation. These authors define aesthetic judgement as a "sensory-affective disclosure of merit" (ibid.: 113), and by merit they mean a feeling that presents and is responsive to an object that is worthy of being liked. The distinguishing feature of aesthetic reasons is that they are reasons for feeling a certain way. The basic insight of this view is that because aesthetic judgement involves appreciation, all aesthetic judgements are perceptual and rational. In other words, unlike blind sensation, aesthetic liking has a cognitive capability insofar as it constitutes an experience in which the world reveals itself to us. The experiential nature of aesthetics means that aesthetic liking has the power to reveal the world immediately rather than mediately.

Shrivastava et al. (2017) argue that one of the main reasons behind the relative lack of regard for ethical and environmental issues on the part of management is the absence of appreciation of aesthetic processes. They point out that *aesthetic rationality* influences every aspect and every level of organizational intervention and is a required complement to the instrumental conception of organization. They argue that aesthetic experiences occur commonly in organizations and that emotions, beliefs, value discourses and aesthetic judgements are part of every member's "seemingly objective" (ibid.: 381) decision-making practices. Shrivastava and colleagues put forward that the non-rational aspects of aesthetics operate "in duality" (ibid.: 381) with cognitive rationality, and suggest a methodology for investigating the process of how daily organizational events create an ethic-aesthetic environment in the organization.

The process starts with an emotive response, created when an individual has an aesthetic experience and instinctively draws on his/her moral values. Once it is acknowledged that the person is in the presence of an ethical issue, she/he naturally forms a judgement based on her/his own experience. Next, interpretive reasoning and social discourse involving rational communication of the experience take place, operating at both emotional and cognitive levels. Finally, collective meaning is achieved as the outcome of communicated reason, and this happens through the mutual understanding of the shared aesthetic experience. Thus, the process of aesthetic rationality involves *both* the interaction between moral intuitions and sensory knowledge, *and* dialogue, which is associated with cognition and rational analysis. Moreover, in their argument towards developing a sensitivity for sustainability, Shrivastava et al. put forward that aesthetic rationality has a relevant role in "initiating a dialogue about the universal importance of social and natural concerns" (ibid.: 385). A remark that provides an additional contribution to our argument about the need to reposition organizations design as the new "conscience" behind the organization's social and environmental responsibilities.

MacIntyre's Virtue Ethics

Virtues is an approach to ethics developed by Alasdair MacIntyre, one of the best known contemporary moral philosophers. MacIntyre's work has been influential influence across the social sciences, including organization studies, where it has been applied by authors such as Beadle and Moore (2006), Mangham (1995), Moore (2002), More (2012), Moore and Grandy (2017) or Tsoukas (2018). Rather than defining ethics as sets of rules to tell right from wrong, that author proposes a theory centred on virtues. He defines virtues as:

> those dispositions which will not only sustain practices and enable us to achieve the goods internal to practices, but which will sustain us in the relevant kind of quest for the good, by enabling us to overcome the harms, dangers, temptations and distractions which we encounter, and which will furnish us with increasing self-knowledge and increasing knowledge of the good. (MacIntyre 2007: 219)

Notwithstanding the opacity of the quote, we are left with the idea that virtues are something that the world needs and that at the individual level, the more we are able to develop our moral dispositions, the better able we will be to overcome the temptations encountered at every step to act unethically. Virtues are dispositions developed through habituation and refer to what we as humans need to do in order to live a productive and socially useful life. Virtue is the translation of Aristotle's term *arête*, a term that might be understood as "excellence" in today's lingo (Tsoukas 2018). *Arête* is of two types: character (or moral) virtues (e.g., justice, courage, generosity,) and intellectual virtues, where the former are the virtues that human beings need to correct their innate weaknesses and improve their natural strengths. For example, if a woman is said to be honest, this means that she has acquired a disposition to behave honestly in whatever situation she finds herself in. And given that habituation implies the development of both moral sensibilities and affective capabilities, character virtues enable people to relate spontaneously to situations as they happen (Tsoukas 2018).

Inspired by the virtue ethics framework, Moore and Grandy (2017) describe organizations as combinations of practice–institution. Practices provide the focal point of the moral dimension of organizational life, and they are defined as follows:

> any coherent and complex form of socially established cooperative human activity through which goods internal to that form of activity are realized in the course of trying to achieve those standards of excellence which are appropriate to, and partially definitive of, that form of activity. (MacIntyre 2007: 187)

Internal goods refer to the excellence of the products or services and the perfection of the practitioners in the process, given that perfection "might more naturally be taken as referring to the development of the moral character, or the flourishing, of practitioners" (Moore and Grandy 2017: 149). Thus, it is in practices that practitioners exercise virtues in the production of internal goods, and it is the excellence of such goods and the "perfection" of process execution that the potential to contribute to the good of the community lies. External goods lie outside of a person's mind, character or body, and include things like payments, prizes, wealth or political power. They serve the integrity of practices and their internal *goods*, and are typically objects of competition, where there must be winners and losers, unlike the internal goods, where the goal is the achievement of good for the whole community. Institution, on the other hand, is the counterpart of practice. They are bodies of practice, which use external goods to bring people into particular practices, providing everything the practice needs to exist. However, institutions comprise elements that work against the aims of practice, i.e., "they are structured in terms of power and status, and they distribute money, power and status as rewards" (MacIntyre 2007: 194). Therefore, there is constant tension between the practice and the institution and hence between the pursuit of virtue and the forces that oppose virtue.

This brief sketch of MacIntyre's virtue ethics framework serves to highlight a perspective on organizational ethics focused on the character and motivations of the individual member of the organization and on her or his ability to pursue excellence through virtuous performances. Dobson (2004) calls this an agent-based approach and distinguishes it from rules-based approaches focused on standards and guidelines, which are aimed at directing or constraining behaviour in organizations. In the agent-based approach, ethics is contextual in the sense that it is linked to a given member and her circumstances, rather than the adherence to a set of abstract rules contained in a code of ethics. This type of approach bypasses the moral conundrum of rules-based approaches, and the situation where an efficient and rule-abiding professional might be an unethical professional.

Dobson's Ethic-Aesthetic Theory of Business

In his application of virtue ethics to business, Dobson (2007, 2010, 2022) proposes a new theory of business, with aesthetics at its centre. He explains that in the last few decades organizations are immersed in business-originated aesthetic stimuli, like logos, brands, products, advertising, architecture, while the senses of organizational members are flooded by similar stimuli, in and outside of the organization. Borrowing from Heidegger, he suggests that members are "thrown" into multiple aesthetic relations with the organization. Aesthetic relations can be understood as emotional or affective links established between the individual and myriad aspects of her environment. They are the basis of the organization's "aesthetic style", which Dobson (2010) defines as "the essence of the aesthetic relations [the organization] invokes" (ibid.: 396). He explains styles as the essence of an aesthetic theory of the firm, in the sense that style provides "a unified and intense force that permeates (...) [the firm's] myriad aesthetic relations" (ibid.: 396), and clarifies the word "permeate", by saying that it should be interpreted as "flavour" (in the culinary sense). Moreover, Dobson discusses the concept of aesthetic style as having an organizing capability, which enables the firm to project itself and attract stakeholders

Dobson proposes an extension to the traditional theory of the firm, based on fundamental assumptions about the impact of the firm on the world. He suggests that rather than a nexus of simple contractual relations among individuals (Jensen and Meckling 1976) serving various human needs (economic, psychological, social, etc), the firm exists primarily in a nexus of aesthetic relations. According to Dobson (2010), the fundamental relations that define the firm (or the organization) are aesthetic, in the sense that the firm emerges as the result of its "immediate sensory impact on individuals" (ibid.: 399), which leads to the argument that the aesthetic approach precedes and includes the economic and social approaches. By tapping into the most fundamental sensory level of human needs, the primacy of the aesthetic naturally connects with virtues and with the search for virtuosity that should lead the activity of man (MacIntyre 2007). Building on his articulation of the concept of the aesthetic firm, Dobson not only develops the connection with virtues, but also brings a novel interpretation of virtue ethics to be applied to business and/or organizations.

According to traditional interpretation of virtue ethics (Beadle and Moore 2006; Moore and Grandy 2017), it is through virtuous activity within communal practices that people contribute towards the institution's increased efficiency. Therefore, in the traditional approach the dominant idea is that ethics in the form of practices and virtues is entirely aligned with the economic aims of business. However, Dobson (2022) suggests that this understanding and application of virtue ethics to business is somewhat biased, because rather than addressing virtues per se, it makes virtues and their attainment conditional upon the achievement of institutional effectiveness. To better understand this issue, let us go back to practice as the virtue ethics concept discussed above. Indeed, firms only exist if their practices run efficiently, and this, in turn, depends on how committed organizational members are towards excellence in the execution of the firm's practices. Accordingly, the excellence of the practice is the aim, "so that not only is there a good product, but the craftsperson is perfected through and in her or his activity" (MacIntyre 1994, cited by Dobson 2022: 500). This conflates practice with the aims of the organization, but not necessarily with the individual's objectives towards a more virtuous life.

To address the problem, Dobson (2022) argues, in an organizational setting the defining characteristic of practices should lie beyond excellence and should instead be defined by a nurturing capacity for reflection, i.e., "some activity—either individual or collective—that, although similar to the traditional practices of virtue ethics, is true to the pursuit of and fidelity to *aesthetic quality*" (ibid.: 500, italics added). By conceiving the firm as primarily aesthetic in both nature and purpose, Dobson explains that the firm's aesthetic presenting in the world, and its nurturing of reflective practices of aesthetic quality become primary tasks. Such practices are discussed in the case of British Airway's tail fin decoration in the 1990s reflecting the indigenous cultures of many of its destinations, and the case of Reebok athletic shoe division, where innovation is spurred by moral reflection about racial identity and equity. The aim of these examples is to show how organizations will benefit from providing the space for aesthetics-imbued reflective practices, from which ethical messages can be elicited.

Summing up. By definition, a business practice lies within the realm of economic activity and is necessarily tied to economic interests, but in the traditional application of virtue ethics to business there is no space for practitioners—as autonomous individuals—to dwell on the nature and purpose of their role, and in accordance with their own ethic and aesthetic principles. To overcome this, Dobson proposes that a phenomenological space of aesthetic reflection, a space where practitioners can ponder the possibilities of action within each novel situation, is required. Virtue ethics affords organizations moral direction, but it fails to provide a space for reflection outside the institutional realm, "a space necessary to counter meta-physical prejudices, rogue-practices, and the corrupting power of the institution" (ibid.: 499). Hence, self-reflection fills the gap of a purely aesthetic perspective on the firm, which lacks the ability to ground the organization with a moral purpose.

References

Baldessarelli, G., I. Stigliani, and K.D. Elsbach. 2022. The Aesthetic Dimension of Organizing: A Review and Research Agenda. *Academy of Management Annals* 16: 217–257.

Beadle, R., and G. Moore. 2006. MacIntyre on Virtue and Organization. *Organization Studies* 27: 323–340.

Beyes, T., and C. Steyaert. 2012. Spacing Organization: Non-representational Theory and Performing Organizational Space. *Organization* 19 (1): 45–61.

Bourdieu, P. 1990. *The Logic of Practice*. Cambridge: Polity Press.

Dobson, J. 2004. Applying Virtue Ethics to Business: The Agent-Based Approach. *EJBO Electronic Journal of Business Ethics and Organization Studies* 9 (1). Retrieved from http://ejbo.jyu.fi.

Dobson, J. 2007. Aesthetics as a Foundation for Business Activity. *Journal of Business Ethics* 72: 41–46.

Dobson, J. 2010. Aesthetic Style as a Postructural Business Ethic. *Journal of Business Ethics* 93: 393–400.

Dobson, J. 2022. Virtue Ethics, Aesthetics, and Reflective Practices in Business. *Philosophy of Management* 21. 493–505.

Gherardi, S. 2016. To start practice theorizing anew: the contribution of the concepts of agencement and formativeness. *Organization*, 23 (5): 680–698

Gorodeisky, K., and E. Marcus. 2018. Aesthetic Rationality. *Journal of Philosophy* 115 (3): 113–140.

Jensen, M., and W.H. Meckling. 1976. Theory of the Firm: Managerial Behaviour, Agency Costs, and Ownership Structure. *Journal of Financial Economics* 3 (4): 305 360.

Ladkin, D. 2018. The Aesthetic and its Relationship to Business Ethics: philosophical underpinnings and implications for future research. *Journal of Business Ethics*, 147: 35–51

Levinson, J. 1998. Aesthetics and Ethics. In *Aesthetics and Ethics: Essays at the Intersection*, ed. J. Levinson, 1–25. Cambridge: Cambridge University Press.

MacIntyre, A. 1994. A Partial Response to My Critics. In *After MacIntyre*, ed. J. Horton and S. Mendus. Cambridge: Polity Press.

MacIntyre, A. 2007. *After Virtue*, 3rd ed. London: Duckworth.

Mangham, I. L. 1995. Macintyre and the Manager. *Organization*, 2 (2): 181–204

Moore, G. 2002. On the Implications of the Practice-Institution Distinction: MacIntyre and the Application of Modern Virtue Ethics to Business. *Business Ethics Quarterly* 12 (1): 19–32.

Moore, G. 2012. The Virtue of Governance, the Governance of Virtue. *Business Ethics Quarterly* 22 (2): 293–318.

Moore, G., and G. Grandy. 2017. Bringing Morality Back In: Institutional Theory and MacIntyre. *Journal of Management Inquiry* 26 (2): 146–164.

Reckwitz, A. 2012. Affective Spaces: A Praxeological Outlook. *Rethinking History* 16 (2): 241–258.

Reckwitz, A. 2017. Practices and Their Affects. In *The Nexus of Practices: Connections, Constellations, and Practitioners*, ed. S. Hui, E. Shove, and T. Schatzki, 114–125. London: Routledge.

Shrivastava, P., G. Schumacher, D.M. Wasieleski, and M. Tasic. 2017. Aesthetic Rationality in Organizations: Toward Developing a Sensitivity for Sustainability. *The Journal of Applied Behavioural Science* 53 (3): 369–411.

Shusterman, R.M. 2004. Pragmatism and East-Asian Thought. *Metaphilosophy* 35 (1/2): 13–43.

Shusterman, R.M. 2009. The Convergence of Ethics and Aesthetics: A Genealogical, Pragmatist Perspective. In *The Hand and the Soul: Ethics and Aesthetics in Architecture and Art*, ed. S. Iliescu. Charlottesville, VA: University of Virginia Press.

Strati, A. 2015. Aesthetics and Design: An Epistemology of the Unseen. In *The Routledge Companion to Philosophy in Organization Studies*, ed. R. Mir, H. Willmott, and M. Greenwood, 251–259. London: Routledge.

Taylor, S.S., and H. Hansen. 2005. Finding Form: Looking at the Field of Organizational Aesthetics. *Journal of Management Studies* 42 (6): 1211–1231.

Thrift, N. 2000. Afterwords. *Environment and Planning D: Society and Space* 18 (2): 213–255.

Thrift, N. 2008. *Non-representational Theory: Space, Politics, Affect*. London: Routledge.

Tsoukas, H. 2018. Strategy and Virtue: Developing Strategy-as-Practice Through Virtue Ethics. *Strategic Organization* 16 (3): 323–351.
Warren, S. 2008. Empirical Challenges in Organizational Aesthetics Research: Towards a Sensual Methodology. *Organization Studies* 29 (4): 559–580.

PART II

The New Approach

The traditional intellectual scaffolding of organization design is contingency theory. This rationale served the discipline well at a time when organization design was seen as an exercise in maximizing performance outcomes while minimizing the misfit between varied environmental demands and internal organizational arrangements (Van de Ven et al. 2014). Although such an instrumental stance is still required, macro and micro environmental conditions have changed beyond recognition and contingency-based formulations can no longer be considered as *the* paradigm for organization design. On the contrary, contingency has become a strait jacket, preventing the discipline from breaking away from the notion of "design" as an objective structural configuration.

The notion of design can be applied and interpreted in several ways, many of which with intangible or immaterial contents, such as, for example, service design, or organization design. In a review of the field, Van de Ven et al. (2014) signal the existence of an emergent school of thought—the Creative Design Perspective—inspired by the recent movement of design thinking and adopting a situated view of organization. In describing the contents of this perspective, Van de Ven et al. submit that "because people are affordant", ongoing design activity leads to "new enactments and affordances of organizing" (Ibid, p. 428, original citations omitted). Indeed, this school of thought reaffirms many of Weick's (2001) arguments about organization design as improvisation, such as the notion that design is continuously reconstructed (rather than constructed at a single point in time), or that an organization has multiple designs (rather than a single design), or that organization design is a recipe (rather than a blueprint) (see also Chapter 2). Instead of structuralist recipes, the new school of thought adopts a more encompassing view of organization design, to include the organizational responsibilities for "the betterment of the human condition" (Jelinek et al., 2008: 317).

The Creative Organization Design school of thought incorporates the sensory, the aesthetic and the creative sides of design (Barry 2011), all contributing towards generative criteria, which transcend the search for efficiency in terms of forms of organizing. Avital and Te'eni (2009) have coined the notion of the organization's design "generative capacity", which is defined as a *personal attribute* that concerns the "ability to reframe reality and subsequently to produce something ingenious or at least new in a particular context" (Ibid, p. 346). This is a major step forward, in the sense that a property of organization at the highest level is being correlated with an organizational property at the individual level, in terms of organization design. One of the challenges for future research direction of this school of thought is the integration of the sensory, the aesthetic and the creative sides of design with the instrumental, the rational and the analytical.

In this book, we contribute to this trend by proposing a new approach founded upon the premise that organizational phenomena result from individual human intentionality, although there is a recognition that natural causes also intervene, independent of intended behaviour (McKelvey 1997). Such a definition of the study of organization, is similar to Simon's (1996) articulation of the problem of design as a school of professional thought that requires "education in both artificial and natural science at a high intellectual level" (Ibid, p. 113). Design science or the design discipline as our preferred designation (Cross 2001) is focused on the creation of systems that do not yet exist or on the improvement of performance of existing systems. In the case of social systems, this is achieved by means of the creation of new social practices or changes in existing ones.

Based on this background, we put forward a new model, which will hopefully not only add to the repertoire of MOS, but also change the existing paradigm of organization design. However, before going into a detailed description of the model, this section proceeds with two topics that are complementary to the main model. The first is a characterization of organizational artefacts as the building blocks of organization design, and a brief discussion about the real difficulties facing any attempt to classify or categorize them. The second is a discussion about the non-unitary nature of organization design and the need to split the concept into levels: the local/operational/technical level and the holistic level, the latter being the book's main theme.

References

Avital, M., and D. Te'eni. 2009. From Generative Fit to Generative Capacity: Exploring an Emerging Dimension of Information Systems Design and Task Performance. *Information Systems Journal* 19: 345–367.

Barry, D. 2011. Re-designing Organization Design. Paper presented at the Design Business Conference, Barcelona, November 17–18.

Cross, N. 2001. Designerly Ways of Knowing: design discipline versus design science. *Design Issues*, 17: 49–55.

Jelinek, M., A.G.L. Romme, and R.J. Boland. 2008. Introduction to the Special Issue Organization Studies as a Science for Design: Creating Collaborative Artifacts and Research. *Organization Studies* 29 (3): 317–329.

McKelvey, B. 1997. Perspective—Quasi-Natural Organization Science. *Organization Science* 8 (4): 351–380.

Simon, H. A. 1996. The Sciences of the Artificial, 3rd edition. Cambridge, MA: MIT Press

Van de Ven, A.H., M. Ganco, and C.B. Hinings. 2014. Returning to the Frontier of Contingency Theory of Organizational and Institutional Designs. *The Academy of Management Annals* 7: 393–440.

CHAPTER 4

Organizational Artefacts

Abstract This chapter is aimed at introducing the topic of organizational artefacts as the primary building blocks or organization design. Artefacts can include colours, dress and accessories, furnishings, buildings, offices, stores, vehicles, windows, cartoons, logos and emblems, as well as the policies, procedures and systems that make the organization function on a daily basis. They are sociomaterial entities and have a profound influence in organizational life by enabling, hindering and even prescribing action, as well as in defining participation and regulating systems, routines and organizational processes. Artefacts can be described in terms of types, functions or extent of contribution to organizational meanings, i.e., they can be considered in terms of the meanings for the people who design, create or implement them, for the people who use or are affected by them, for the participants in organizational interactions occurring in daily organizational life, and for external stakeholders when interacting with the organization. From this very brief description, it is clear that the diversity of perspectives on artefacts in organizations is enormous and for the reason the topic will not be developed in any depth. However, the chapter has an important message for the remainder of the book, i.e., given that all interactions, relationships and experiences that form the organization's design are *mediated* by organizational artefacts, the way we design artefacts is crucial for everything the organization wishes to do, including its ethical positioning on social, corporate governance and environmental issues.

R. Magalhães, *Designing Organizations for the Betterment of Society*,
https://doi.org/10.1007/978-3-031-64483-2_4

Keywords Artefact functions · Artefact types · Mediation · Organizational artefact · Organizational meanings · Sociomateriality

As mentioned earlier, we follow the premise that organizations are complex social artefacts where the rules for the artificial intermingle with the rules for the natural and the social. What this means is that a suitable framework for theorizing organization design *must* combine principles from the sciences of the artificial (i.e., design) with principles from the social sciences. For the social sciences, organizations are enacted constructs in which structure, meaning and culture co-evolve (Bate et al. 2000; Weick 1979). For the sciences of design, organizations are artefacts, which, according to Simon (1996: 5), are artificial creations that:

i. are synthesized (though not always or usually with full forethought) by human beings
ii. can be characterized in terms of functions, goals, and adaptation
iii. are often discussed, particularly when they are being designed, in terms of imperatives as well as descriptives.

Seen in this light, artefacts are creations by people and for people. Indeed, in the organization everything that enables it to function are artefacts. From its mission and vision to the systems and procedures that guide its horizontal processes, from the hierarchical rules that ensure its command and control and from the products to the services that ensure its survival, the entirety of the organization's life depends on the design and execution of a pervasive and ever-evolving *infrastructure of artefacts*. However, artefacts are not only intentional products of human action which exist independently of their creator, but they are also entities with their own corporality perceived by the senses and interpreted by the people who deploy, use or evaluate them. Although they go unnoticed by most people in organizations, artefacts play a key role in organizational change, "since everyday life is characterized by an inexhaustible process of interpreting, inventing and reshaping forms by its participants" (Strati, 2015: 56).

Artefacts can include colours, dress and accessories, furnishings, buildings, offices, stores, vehicles, windows, cartoons, logos and emblems and more (Vilnai-Yavetz and Rafaeli 2005), and they can be used to signify and influence identity, to enact group membership and status, or to construct and embody organizational knowledge (Bechky 2008). Macpherson et al. (2010) suggest that organizational artefacts can be used to create and sustain discourse and dialogue among organizational actors, to define participation or norms that regulate systems or routines, to define or re-define organizational space or time, or to create political leverage and politicize organizational processes. Gagliardi (2006) explains that artefacts are primary cultural phenomena, with a profound influence in organizational life by enabling, hindering and even prescribing action. They are capable of structuring sensory experience, and often work as "clues" to ways of doing, seeing and feeling. Hence, when considering artefacts as the building blocks or organization design, one needs to take into account not only the material properties of the artefact, but also the fact that they are inherently sociomaterial (Orlikowski 2009).

Although several authors talk about the expression ***organizational artefacts***, there is no universally recognized classification or framework either in MOS or design research. Jelinek et al. (2008) suggest a comprehensive list of artefacts, which covers most of the concerns of a holistic understanding of organization design (ibid.: 321):

- Products (as the end results of a manufacturing process)
- Goods, services and identities (as artifacts to be traded and sold)
- Structures (signaling the sequence of authority levels and the distribution of task domains)
- Management tools and systems (created as instruments for accomplishing certain managerial intentions)
- Human–machine interfaces (the artifacts that mediate between computers or airplanes and their users)
- Multi-user systems and networks (the artefacts that facilitate the coordination of many human activities across time and space)
- Projects and programs (e. g., a new product development project or an employee empowerment program)
- Discourses (semantic systems or narratives around a professional routine, role model, or ideology).

The above listing of artefact types suggests a number of artefact functions that may be applicable to a definition of organization design as an artificial creation made up of myriad artefacts fulfilling different functions and roles. The range of functions is immense, but an attempt to simplify the categorization suggests no more than five basic functions:

- Control
- Coordination
- Communication
- Influence
- Service.

The control and coordination functions are more typical of artefacts concerning internal needs, such as structures or management systems. The communication and influence functions characterize artefacts aimed at the environment, such as corporate identity or product brand. The service function characterizes artefacts that are outputs of the organization's activity and applies to both products and services (Vargo and Lusch 2004, 2008). The service function straddles both the internal and external focus because all organizational outputs affect the perception of the organization's design, for example, the reputation or image associated with a product or a service has a bearing not only on market share, but also on the commitment and loyalty of internal stakeholders. The influence function is typically more prevalent in artefacts aimed at the outside world, but it can also have a bearing on internal cohesion, for example, through leadership, a discourse artefact. Some artefacts may have characteristics of several functions; for example, a customer relationship management system is an example of an artefact with both internal (coordination) and external focus (communication).

Having highlighted the possibilities and difficulties inherent in attempting to describe organizational artefacts, in terms of types and functions, there must also be a word about methodology. Inspired by literature on design science, Pandza & Thorpe (2010) suggest three different approaches to the design and construction of organizational artefacts. The first type is deterministic design, an approach based on managerial intention, according to which design decisions determine the designed artefacts and their subsequent behavior. Also known as engineering design, this approach is viewed, first and foremost, as a problem-solving activity that leads to an optimal design solution. The second is path-dependent design, an approach that highlights the role of evolution and the fact that design process depends on evolutionary processes concerned with factors such as, knowledge accumulation, learning, or adaptation. The third approach is labelled path-creation design, an approach that acknowledges the role of agency in the design process, as well as the high level of complexity in the process of social artefact construction.

Whereas deterministic design places the expert designer at centre-stage in the design process, path-dependent design acknowledges the evolutionary emergence of the artefacts, with the designer playing a passive role responding adaptively to the incremental progression of the artefact. According to path-dependent approaches, the organizational designer is limited to accepting and adopting the interpretation made by the expert of the design principles or rules to be applied and prevented from exploring uncertainty and finding novelty and uniqueness. The third approach–path-creation–diverges significantly from the status-quo of traditional artefact methodologies and is closely aligned to Krippendorff's (2006) notion of design, where the mission is to create the conditions for the emergence of novelty. This approach is wholly non-deterministic, acknowledging the agency of individual designers in actively shaping the emergence and evolution of artefacts and creating radically new knowledge.

Artefact Roles and Categories of Organizational Meanings

The agency of individual designers emphasized by path-creating artefact methodologies requires an understanding of the notion of organization design-as-meaning, in the sense that organizational artefacts can be seen as having different meanings, depending on their role or their stage of development. We suggest four different categories of meaning as a contribution towards the management of artefacts in organizations:

i. the meanings of organizational artefacts for the people who design, create or implement them (decision-makers, product designers, systems analysts, etc.);
ii. the meanings of organizational artefacts for the people using or affected by them (including internal and external artefacts);
iii. the emergent meanings for participants in (artefact-mediated or artefact-impacted) organizational interactions occurring in task execution, routine performance or daily organizational life;

iv. the meanings for internal and external organizational stakeholders of organizational experiences associated or not with the mediation or impact of organizational artefacts.

The four categories of organization design-related meanings represent a progression from artefact-specific to organization-wide meanings, in an accumulation of different methods of organization designing. As it can be seen in Fig. 4.1, the first category concerns the meanings of artefacts for the designer or the manager who decides to create the artefact. The second category of meaning is emergent and concerns the meanings of organizational artefacts for the people using or in any way affected by them. The third category encompasses the meanings contained in interactions in any way mediated or impacted by artefacts and occurring during task execution, routine performance or daily organizational life. The fourth category concerns meanings of the organization as a whole to include the sum total of the effects of artefact mediation,[1] leadership style, interaction patterns and cultural influences on organizational experience understood as the outcome of not only processes of rational or intellectual sensemaking, but also of non-cognitive or sensory ones, such as emotion, affect or intuition.

The above descriptions of artefact types, functions and contributions to organizational meanings are not meant to be exhaustive or comprehensive; instead, they are intended to provide the reader with an idea of the huge *diversity of perspectives* on artefacts in organizations. Given that each type of artefact has its own jargon and its own methods, and that most large and medium-sized organizations choose to outsource the design, development, maintenance and sometimes operation of many of their artefacts (for example, IT artefacts), it is not feasible to think of the infrastructure of organizational artefacts as something that can be standardized or centrally controlled within the organization. With the exception of standard company logos, mottos or graphics, and a few other

[1] By mediation we mean the positioning of the artefact between the person and the task. In other words, for organizational members to carry out their tasks, they use artefacts, which means that the way the task is accomplished depends on the artefact. In organization design, mediation is important because the way that artefacts are designed will affect the way people work, interact and create relationships.

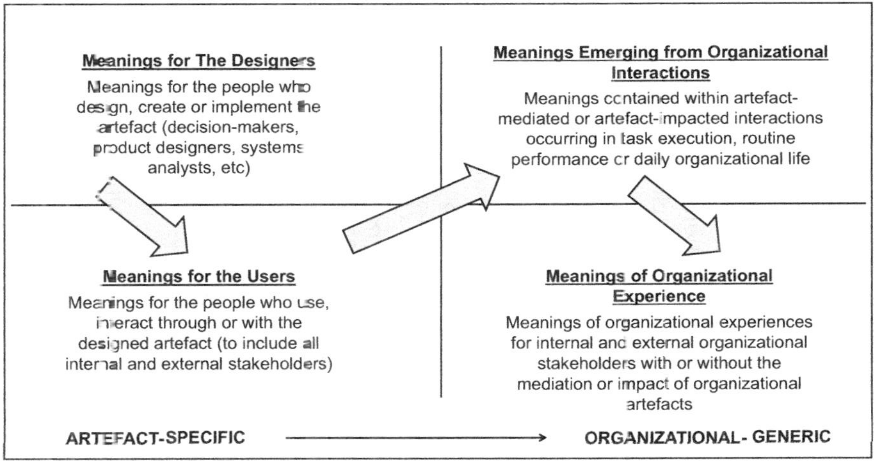

Fig. 4.1 The role of organizational artefacts in shaping organizational meanings: From single artefacts at the local level to the design of the organization as a holistic artefact

artefacts that can be centrally controlled, the process of designing organizational artefacts has to be managed locally and can only be steered from a higher level.

Hence, the study of organizational artefacts within the realm of organization design holds a conundrum: on one hand, it cannot be divorced from the wider theme of designing organizations, because each artefact plays a role in the overall design, but on the other hand, organizational artefacts are too diverse to fit into a definition of organization as a holistic identifiable entity. Moreover, ***intentional design*** implies a degree of control over the entity being designed. So, for organizations to be able to coordinate their infrastructure of organizational artefacts without interfering with the design and implementation of each artefact or group of artefacts at the local level, they need to develop a governance mechanism at a higher level. Jelinek et al. (2008: 324) suggest a set of "principles that are context-specific and infused with interpretations, expectations, roles and relationships that matter". We will return to this suggestion further on in the book.

References

Bate, P., R. Khan, and A. Pye. 2000. Towards a Culturally Sensitive Approach to Organizational Structuring: Where Organization Design Meets Organization Development. *Organization Science* 11 (2): 197–211.

Bechky, B.A. 2008. Analyzing Artifacts: Material Methods for Understanding Identity, Status, and Knowledge in Organizational Life. In *The SAGE Handbook of New Approaches in Management and Organization*, ed. D. Barry and H. Hansen. London: Sage.

Gagliardi, P. 2006. Exploring the Aesthetic Side of Organizational Life. In *The Sage Handbook of Organizations Studies*, ed. S.R. Clegg, C. Hardy, T.B. Lawrence, and W.R. Nord. London: Sage.

Jelinek, M., A.G.L. Romme, and R.J. Boland. 2008. Introduction to the Special Issue Organization Studies as a Science for Design: Creating Collaborative Artifacts and Research. *Organization Studies* 29 (3): 317–329.

Krippendorff, K. 2006. The Semantic Turn: a new foundation for design. Boca Raton, FL: Taylor and Francis.

Macpherson, A., A. Kofinas, O. Jones, and R. Thorpe. 2010. Making Sense of Mediated Learning: Cases from Small Firms. *Management Learning* 41 (3): 303–323.

Orlikowski, W.J. 2009. The Sociomateriality of Organisational Life: Considering Technology in Management Research. *Cambridge Journal of Economics* 34: 125–141.

Pandza, K., Thorpe, R. 2010. Management as Design but What Kind of Design? An Appraisal of the Design Science Analogy for Management. *British Journal of Management* 21 (1): 171–186 https://doi.org/10.1111/bjom.2010.21.issue-110.1111/j.1467-8551.2008.00623.x

Simon, H.A. 1996. *The Sciences of the Artificial*, 3rd ed. Cambridge, MA: MIT Press.

Strati, A. 2015. "Aesthetics and Design: an epistemology of the unseen". In R. Mir, H. Willmott & M. Greenwood, ed., *The Routledge Companion to Philosophy in Organization Studies*, pp. 251–259. London: Routledge.

Vargo, S.L., and R.F. Lusch. 2004. Evolving to a New Dominant Logic for Marketing. *Journal of Marketing* 68: 1–17.

Vargo, S.L., and R.F. Lusch. 2008. Service-Dominant Logic: Continuing the Evolution. *Journal of the Academy of Marketing Science* 36: 1–10.

Vilnai-Yavetz, I., and A. Rafaeli. 2005. Managing Organizational Artifacts to Avoid Artifact Myopia. In *Artifacts and Organizations: Beyond Mere Symbolism*, ed. A. Rafaeli and M. Pratt. London: Psychology Press.

Weick, K.E. 1979. *The Social Psychology of Organizing*, 2nd ed. Reading, MA: Addison-Wesley.

CHAPTER 5

The Case for Organization Design as a Non-unitary Construct

Abstract In this chapter, it is argued that organization design should not continue to be treated as a unitary construct as was the case with organization design-as-structure. Instead, based on Barnard's (The Functions of the Executive. Harvard University Press, Cambridge, MA, 1938) managerial theory of organization, we suggest that for different stages in the entrepreneurial/managerial process different management approaches are required, i.e., a stage focused on the efficiency of detail and a stage emphasizing the "creative economy of the whole". Hence, in the light of two well-known management topics—management control systems and dynamic capabilities—we suggest that the construct of organization design should also be split into two levels of analysis/intervention: the *local/operational/technical* and the *holistic*. The operational level tends to be technical in nature and concerns the design and operation of organizational artefacts aimed at supporting the efficient and effective creation of value at the local level. The upper level is suggested as a ***holistic concern*** that applies non-rational, non-analytical and holistic lenses to management problems. In the case of management control systems, the whole takes the form of a logic of *loose coupling*, while in the case of capability theory, the holistic solution is known as *dynamic capability*.

Keywords Barnard · Dynamic capability · Holistic · Local · Loose coupling · Management accounting · Management control · Operational · Technical

R. Magalhães, *Designing Organizations for the Betterment of Society*,
https://doi.org/10.1007/978-3-031-64483-2_5

Tracking Organization Design in Two Well-Known Management Problem Areas—Management Accounting and Organizational Capabilities

Management Accounting

From the traditional viewpoint, organization design is understood as the outcome of managerial decision-making, in the pursuance of the organization's strategic objectives. It reflects a top-down posture of intentionality starting with the setting up of the formal organizational structure, which is subsequently broken down in terms of a wide array of control *artefacts*, ranging from high-level managerial policies to a variety of procedural and feedback systems. This is the perspective that is traditionally taught to students of management and that has been reinforced, over the years, by the influential accounting community. As it can be seen in Fig. 5.1, in an application of contingency theory similar to traditional organization design, management accounting is founded upon the premise that organization design (i.e., structure, shape, centralization, interdependencies, etc.) is a simple step in a unidirectional process of organizational control leading to the setting up of accounting systems. According to this perspective, organization design is something quite static that happens very occasionally in the life of the organization.

Figure 5.1 also conveys the belief that it was possible to control the organization through a single "organizational control package", an

Fig. 5.1 Traditional management control/ performance perspective on organization design (*Source* Otley 1980)

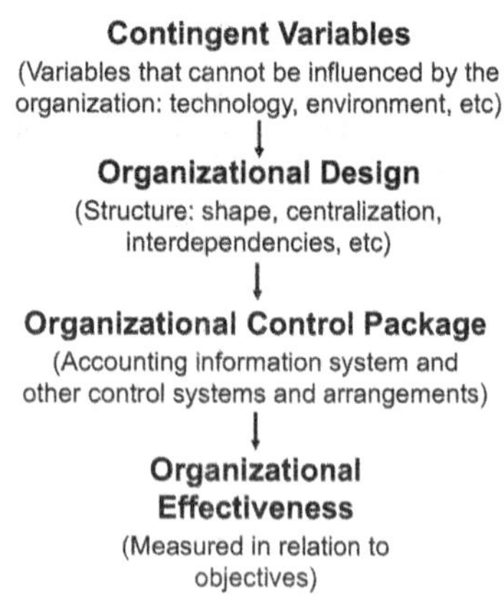

assumption that has been thrown into question by the widespread deployment of modular control systems by departmental or functional units in every type of organization (Otley 2016; Merchant and Otley 2020). This technological advance has caused major problems of loss of control and poor integration of resources across the organization. Demartini and Otley's (2020) research on the topic suggests that the solution may lie in a compromise between centralization and decentralization, in the form of organizational control systems made up by loosely coupled components. The authors suggest that loose coupling provides a balance between some flexibility for local control and the need for overall coordination, while affording the organization with the highest possible levels of managerial effectiveness and process innovation.

Thus, if the organization's design can be assumed to be not a step *before* the setting up of organization level control systems, but the *result* of each and every control system in the organization, an early conclusion that can be taken from this glance at the literature on management control systems is that the concept of organization design would be far more useful if it were to be *split* into two parts: on one hand, the design focused on local/operational efficiency and effectiveness, and on the other hand, design dedicated to the harmonization of the various local interests and priorities, as well as some form of overall coordination.

Organizational Capabilities

Featuring a strong economics bias, dynamic capabilities theory is a trend from the resource-based approach (RBA) to strategy. It focuses on firm-specific capabilities that can be sources of competitive advantage and offers a framework to explain how combinations of competences and resources can be developed, deployed and protected (Teece et al. 1997). Although this school of thought considers organization design as a merely structural issue, it also ponders the possibility that organizational design and organizational capabilities may co-evolve (Kay et al. 2018). Dynamic capabilities are theorized at two levels of abstraction: the level of ordinary capabilities, commonly represented by indicators such as labour productivity, inventory turns, or industry best practices, which on their own are not sufficient to produce competitive differentiation, and a higher level of dynamic capabilities, which enable the enterprise to direct its ordinary activities towards "high-payoff endeavours" (Teece 2014: 328).

Examples of dynamic capabilities are alliancing, strategic decision-making or knowledge brokering (Eisenhardt and Martin 2000). Considering any of these three examples, the first thing that emerges is the difficulty in explaining the performance of lower-level (ordinary) capabilities without referring to the policies, procedures and systems which are a part of the infrastructure of organizational design. However, this literature is ambiguous about the role of organization design, appearing to consider design as something that is both associated with, and distinct from organizational capabilities. For example, Leih et al. (2015) state that "if dynamic capabilities are thought of as a latent construct, organization design is one of several indicator variables" (ibid.: 10), while Augier and Teece (2008) concede that "strategy processes are evolutionary by nature, but they involve significant elements of intentional design and orchestration of assets by managers" (ibid.: 1201). Thus, while strategy and design seem to work in tandem, nobody seems to be able to explain how. Faced with this conundrum, Dosi et al. (2008) suggest that the answer to the issue of organizational capabilities might be found in something similar to the invisible hand of the market, a phenomenon well-known to economists. They state:

> Just as the market system accomplishes remarkable feats of coordination without the aid of a central plan, organizational learning produces the coordinated performances of organizational capabilities without the aid of a recipe or, alternatively, without the aid of a comprehensive plan, optimized or not. According to the mainstream tradition in economics, economic actors do not have to understand the price system for it to work. Similarly, an organization produces coordinated activity *without anyone knowing how it works*. (ibid.: 1178, italics added)

Such comparison with the market system is not dissimilar to the metaphors of "orchestration" and "choreography" (Teece 2007) often used by the capabilities literature. Hence, this suggests that at the highest-level of organizational capabilities it is necessary to consider a level of analysis that goes beyond the realm of the rational and the instrumental and enters the domain of the aesthetic. Indeed, it suggests that the connection between coordination, capabilities and organization design lies at a level variously labelled "meta", "gestalt" or "cultural". In the field of organizational capabilities, this idea was pioneered by Collis (1994) and indeed, Dosi et al. (2008) also agree that coordination is, in fact, produced by the social relations generated by the organization's structures. Nevertheless, despite the choice on the approach to organization design, as a monolith only defined by the properties of the organization's formal structure, the literature does recognize the need to split organizational capabilities into two levels: a lower level focused on achieving operational efficiency and effectiveness, and a higher level, where the concerns are of a more emergent nature, aimed at the maintenance of competitive differentiation.

The Need for a Conceptual Split in the Theorizing of Organization Design(ing)

From the discussion above, we have learned that both the literature on management accounting and on organizational capabilities show that research into the micro level of operational or technical issues has created the need for a higher or macro level of analysis to be articulated. In the case of poor coordination and integration of local control systems, research suggests the need for a new mechanism, inspired by the notion of loose coupling. In the case of organizational capabilities, the emergent need is for a conceptual framework that can accommodate the notions of choreography or orchestration of ordinary capabilities. Both cases can be seen as organization design problems, but they have not been recognized as such. Traditionally, organization design has been conceptualized as a structural monolith, and although such a belief has been countered by the writings of several authors, including Weick's, the traditional mindset has endured. Weick (2001) suggests that organization design is not a *unitary quality* of organization, and that it should instead be seen as an assembly of many designs.

More recently and writing from an intellectual background quite different from Weick's social constructionism, Puranam (2018) also questions the unitary perspective. Arguing from a definition of organization designing as "the search for solutions to the universal problems of organizing" (ibid.: 21), that author defends the need to make the distinction between macro- and micro-organizational designs. He explains the "universal problems of organizing" as the problems of classic organization design theory, i.e., division of labour, task allocation, information or incentives, all derived from the principle of hierarchical organization. According to Puranam, these issues remain constant at any level of aggregation, and they relate to how the efforts of organization members are aggregated at all levels of analysis, from teams on the shop floor to teams on board rooms, or from strategic alliances to consortia between firms.

While concurring with the view that organization design is not a unitary quality of organization and that there should be a distinction between levels of organization designing, we do not share Puranam's views either on the essence of the phenomenon of organizing, or on the nature of aggregation from the micro to the macro levels. Puranam uses the term "organizing" without explaining what it means, ignoring that in the MOS literature, the essence of organizing has been persuasively spelled out by Weick (1969, 1979, 1995) as the ongoing attempt to achieve coordinated action through sensemaking. Sensemaking is explained as the human ability to structure unknown contexts or actions and assigning them with meaning, which in turn means that organization emerges out of processes of sensemaking and organizing. This is achieved through a progressive reduction of equivocality among the participants in the organizing processes, with common understandings being shared among them, and resulting in order (i.e., organization) becoming established. Hence, if one is to use the term "organizing" in the way that it has been expounded by Weick, then the discussion will move away from the purely instrumental purpose of structuring organizations hierarchically, and from the belief that designing organizations is simply a process whereby rational actors execute strategic plans to meet organizational goals.

As regards the nature of aggregation from the micro to the macro levels, Puranam (2018) does not suggest any social mechanism but proposes, without explaining how, that the two levels are linked by abstract principles of hierarchy, supposedly applicable to different levels of analysis. The boundaries of the construct of micro-structure are defined in a vague manner and ranging between something as simple as a team of workers and the bewildering complexity of a consortium between firms. According to the micro-foundation movement in MOS (Felin et al., 2015), the link between the micro to the macro levels needs to be justified and supported by extant literature on social organization. Thus, we submit that issue of the non-unitary nature of organization design needs to be addressed; however, it needs to be done with the support of the literature on social organization, and there is a good number of choices, such as sensemaking, structuration or organizational culture, the choices we have made to describe the phenomenon of organization design.

Organization Design: One -Off or Never Ending?

Although the traditional understanding of organization design is portrayed in most textbooks as an infrequent exercise for creating organizational structures, organization design happens at every step of the way in the daily lives of managers and whenever they make decisions that result in the creation or alteration of organizational systems or procedures. Such decisions are design decisions and to support them a huge variety of "design methodologies". Most design methodologies are modelled upon the Simonian notion that design "problems" need to be broken down into smaller and manageable parts, so that solutions (usually modular) can be found and offered. Such design activity is often conducted by management consulting firms and, although it does not usually appear in management textbooks as part of the topic of organization design, in the consulting community the activity is clearly labelled "organization design" (see, for example, Visscher and Visscher-Voerman 2010).

On the other hand, organizational design is also referred to as a platform, a meta-capability or a perennial and incomplete activity. This idea is inspired by Simon's notion of the design of social organizations as something without end goals, and as part of the task of "configuring organizations" (Simon 1996: 154). In this important contribution to organizational design, the question of end goals arises because designing of social organizations is severely limited by designers' inability to represent the design problem or to predict the future. Such an insight has been acknowledged in organization design research (Garud et al. 2008), as well as in the field of service design, where is argued that rather than service design, we should be talking of designing *for* services (Kimbell, 2011). The author explains:

> Talking of designing *for* services rather than ***designing services*** recognizes that what is being designed is not an end result, but rather a platform for action with which diverse actors will engage over time. (ibid.: 45, original citations omitted)

In this citation Kimbell (2011) also proposes that the aim is not a measurable end result but a ***platform for action***, which will enable the provision of services, an idea that has equally been echoed in the organization design literature. Organization design has been labelled as a platform or "virtual organizing scheme" by Ciborra (1996), a "meta-capability" by

Snow et al. (2005) or the "design gestalt" by Yoo et al. (2006). The design gestalt is meant as "a virtual capability that combines ideas, values, resources, tools, and people into ensembles that can create and project remarkable artifacts" (ibid.: 228). Platform, meta-capability or gestalt convey the idea that a sort of higher-level mechanism that will ensure the continuity of action over time is required, in order to carry out a design process in an open-ended fashion. However, at the same time, organization designing, understood as the one-off setting up of organizational artefacts, also needs to be factored in.

The Proposal of Organization Design(ing) at Two Levels: The Operational and the Holistic

In thinking about the need to find an acceptable proposal that would fit the *broader context of management/organization theory*, while accommodating the split in the concept of organization design, which has been suggested in the discussion so far about, we have found inspiration in the writings of Barnard (1938). In describing the broad framework on which he bases his managerial theory of organization, he observes that "the final efficiency of organization is dependent upon two quite different factors: (a) the efficiency of detail; and (b) the creative economy of the whole" (ibid.: 253). By the efficiency of detail, Barnard signifies the core managerial activity of controlling costs, output and income, which organizations depend on for their survival. As regards the creative economy of the whole, this is explained as the organization's capacity for coordination, and the basis for the organization as a cooperative system. Coordination, Barnard explains, depends on "creative efficiency", a non-technical capability based on a "sense of things as a whole" and a "persistent subordination of parts to the total" (ibid.: 253). Moreover, he adds that coordination needs to rely on an individual sense of fitness, of proportions, of the appropriate, a type of capacity that relies on *aesthetic* and *moral* judgement, rather than on any rational or analytical capability. This characteristic of the creative economy of the whole is what gives it its innovative and dynamic character.

Barnard's two-factor theory is clearly applicable to organization design. If, as proposed earlier, organization design is theorized as an artefact, which is the outcome of the creation and operation of myriad organizational artefacts, as well as the interactions of people with, through or without the artefacts, the two different levels of analysis emerge with clarity. On one hand, there is a need to consider organization design at an operational/technical level of creation, implementation, operation and change of organizational artefacts, aimed at supporting the efficient and effective creation of knowledge and value at the local level. On the other hand, a higher level must also be considered, a level that would take on board the descriptions of organization design as an ongoing, incomplete platform, or meta-capability, with links to the operational/local/technical level.

Given the huge diversity of artefacts, the higher level should be conceived as something with the characteristics of Barnard's holistic creative efficiency, focused not only on coordination of local artefacts, people and their interactions, but also on the guidance/oversight of the organization's higher purposes. Holistic *coordination* should be understood as a capacity that relies mostly on interactions, relationships, aesthetic and moral judgements. Thus, the higher level of organization design is geared towards the monitoring of performance, not through instrumental analysis, but through the holistic sensing of organizational events and outcomes, and a focus on ethic/aesthetic features. The guidance/oversight of the organization's higher purposes concerns the artefacts being created/operated at the lower level and is aimed at ensuring that artefacts are, *in fact*, contributing to the achievement of the organization's higher purposes.

The Solution Presented by the Two-level Conception of Organization Design to the Unresolved Problems of Management Accounting and Organizational Capabilities

Let us now return to the cases of management accounting and dynamic capabilities as examples of problems, which might have solution in the two-level organization design model proposed in this chapter. In the case of management control, the suggestion from leading researchers in the field is that control systems across the organization can only be loosely coupled (Demartini and Otley 2020). However, we counter that such a solution can only work in cultural contexts where individual actors are capable of cooperating and coordinating across functional borders, and loose coupling should not be seen as a recipe that can be "injected" into the organization. We suggest that the notion of loose coupling should be seen under a broader framework and considered as a holistic organization design problem, the solution for which would need to rely on a culture of cooperation and coordination.

As regards dynamic capabilities, although the nature of the problem is different to the problem of management accounting, the solution applies to both. The problem of dynamic capabilities concerns the synergetic aggregation of capabilities from a level, where the rules of efficiency and effectiveness are well understood, to a higher level where more complex components are involved, and where the *rules of causality no longer apply*. Hence, the problem of dynamic capabilities involves complex answers that fall under the realm of the ethic-aesthetic, rather than the rational-analytic. Taking strategic alliancing as an example of a dynamic capability, the theory suggests that organizations are able to assemble and orchestrate a number of ordinary capabilities, which include not only work-related knowledge and the mediation of several *artefacts*, but also the presence of several other interactional, relational and group-level organizational conditions.

The ability to orchestrate and combine all such components gives the organization superior strategic alliancing capabilities. In other words, when looking at the final outcome, a dynamic capability appears as a complex whole, where components *cannot be prized apart*. Indeed, what this means is that dynamic capabilities require the *entire organization* to be designed in such a way that many different sectors can contribute, including management accounting systems. Hence, it can be concluded that the coordination and cooperation which define the holistic level of organization design encompass *all* the components involved in the formation of the strategic alliancing capability, including cultural, ethic and aesthetic components.

In the light of the two examples above, on the basis of Barnard (1938) two-factor approach—the "efficiency of detail" and the "creative economy of the whole"— and supported by several strands of MOS literature, we suggest that the construct of organization design should also be split into two levels of analysis/intervention: the *local/operational/technical* and the *holistic*. The operational level tends to be technical in nature and concerns the design and operation of organizational artefacts aimed at supporting the efficient and effective creation of value at the local level. Applied to the two examples, the operational level addresses the pursuit for efficiency and effectiveness at the local or departmental level, with a link to the upper level, where the managerial perspective changes to a *holistic posture,* applying a non-rational or non-analytical lens to the issues at hand and coming up with aestho-instrumental assessments.

Concluding

In this chapter, we have argued for the need of a split in the concept of organization design as the starting point of the new approach put forward in this book. Figure 5.2 highlights the central role of the two-level approach to organization design as part of a model of organization as a sociomaterial artefact. Apart from organizational artefacts, which have been discussed in the previous chapter, the remaining components of the model are the higher purposes of the organization and the actions and interactions of the people who make up the organization (i.e., the organization's internal and external stakeholders). The figure assumes, on one hand, a recognition of the strong potential of artefacts to provide form to social interactions, which leads to the proposal that artefacts and their influence on the interactions, relationships and experiences of stakeholders are major drivers of the organization's design (or form). On the other hand, the figure also recognizes the organization's higher purposes (including those with ethical-aesthetic implications) as the source and the benchmark for all designing activity in the organization. If interactions, relationships and experiences are indeed key components of organization design, then it can be assumed that without the contribution from interactions, relationships and experiences of internal and external stakeholders, it will not be possible for management to fully accomplish the organization's purpose.

Unlike strategy, which is open to interpretation and focused on business results, purpose is an all-encompassing foundational statement which defines the organization's identity. For this reason, purpose must be taken as the cornerstone of all organizing activity, and if design is acknowledged as an appropriate normative framework for such activity, then organization design(ing) should be governed by the organization's higher purposes, to include its ethical and aesthetic ambitions. This means that organization design assumes a pivotal role between purpose on one side and interactions, relationships and experiences on the other. Framed in this manner, the definition of organizational design as a two-level mission emerges as the key to an unsolved management problem, i.e., the problem of the link between the level of "efficiency of detail" (local/operational) and

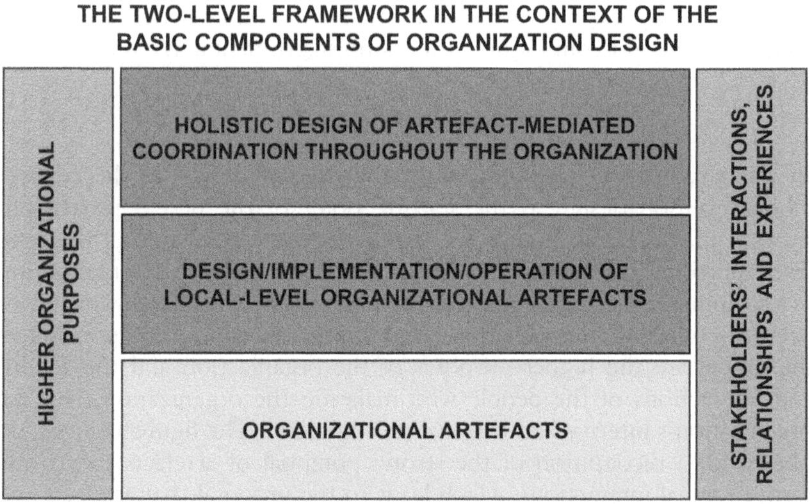

Fig. 5.2 The basic components of organization as an artefact: designing capacity for linking organizational purposes and organizational actions and interactions

the level of "creative economy of the whole" (holistic), after Barnard's (1938) insights.

This perspective presents a unique contribution to organizational theory, in the sense that it offers a framework that allows organizations to combine their business and competitive objectives with their ethical-aesthetic challenges. The dual level designing framework is part and parcel of the *meta-capability* that makes up the organization's design scaffold.

References

Augier, M., and D.J. Teece. 2008. Strategy as Evolution with Design: The Foundations of Dynamic Capabilities and the Role of Managers in the Economic System. *Organization Studies* 29 (08 and 09): 1187–1208.

Barnard, C.I. 1938. *The Functions of the Executive*. Cambridge, MA: Harvard University Press.

Ciborra, C.U. 1996. The Platform Organization: Recombining Strategies, Structures and Surprises. *Organization Science* 7: 103–118.

Collis, D.J. 1994. How Valuable Are Organizational Capabilities? *Strategic Management Journal* 15: 143–152.

Demartini, M.C., and D. Otley. 2020. Beyond the System vs. Package Dualism in Performance Management Systems Design: A Loose Coupling Approach. *Accounting, Organizations and Society* 86: 101072.

Dosi, G., M. Faillo, and L. Marengo. 2008. Organizational Capabilities, Patterns of Knowledge Accumulation and Governance Structures in Business Firms: An Introduction. *Organization Studies* 29: 1165–1185.

Eisenhardt, K.M., and J.A. Martin. 2000. Dynamic Capabilities: What Are They? *Strategic Management Journal* 21: 1105–1121.

Felin, T., N.J. Foss, and R.E. Ployhart. 2015. The Microfoundations Movement in Strategy and Organization Theory. *The Academy of Management Annals* 9 (1): 575–632.

Garud, R., S. Jain, and P. Tuertscher. 2008. Incomplete by Design and Designing for Incompleteness. *Organization Studies* 29: 351–371.

Kay, N.M., S. Leih, and D.J. Teece. 2018. The Role of Emergence in Dynamic Capabilities: A Restatement of the Framework and Some Possibilities for Future Research. *Industrial and Corporate Change* 27 (4): 623–638.

Kimbell, L. 2011. Designing for Service as One Way of Designing Services. *International Journal of Design* 5 (2): 41–52.

Leih, S., G. Linden, and D.J. Teece. 2015. Business Model Innovation and Organizational Design: A Dynamic Capabilities Perspective. In *Business Model Innovation: The Organizational Dimension*, ed. N.J. Foss and T. Saebi. Oxford: Oxford University Press.

Merchant, K.A., and D. Otley. 2020. Beyond the Systems Versus Package Debate. *Accounting, Organizations and Society* 86: 101185.

Otley, D.T. 1980. The Contingency Theory of Management Accounting: Achievement and Prognosis. *Accounting, Organizations and Society* 5 (4): 413–428.

Otley, D.T. 1999. Performance Management: A Framework for Management Control Systems Research. *Management Accounting Research* 10 (4): 363–382.

Otley, D.T. 2016. The Contingency Theory of Management Accounting and Control: 1980–2014. *Management Accounting Research* 31: 45–62.

Puranam, P. 2018. *The Microstructure of Organizations*. Oxford: Oxford University Press.

Simon, H.A. 1996. *The Sciences of the Artificial*, 3rd ed. Cambridge, MA: MIT Press.

Snow, C.C., R.E. Miles, and G. Miles. 2005. A Configurational Approach to the Integration of Strategy and Organization Research. *Strategic Organization* 3 (4): 431–439.

Teece, D.J. 2014. The Foundations of Enterprise Performance: Dynamic and Ordinary Capabilities in an Economic Theory of Firms. *The Academy of Management Perspectives* 28: 328–352.

Teece, D.J., G. Pisano, and A. Shuen. 1997. Dynamic Capabilities and Strategic Management. *Strategic Management Journal* 18: 509–533.

Teece, D.J. 2007. 'Explicating dynamic capabilities: the nature and micro-foundations of (sustainable) enterprise performance'. *Strategic Management Journal* 28: 1319–1350

Visscher, K., Irene, J. & Visscher-Voerman, A. 2010. "Organizational design approaches in management consulting", *Management Decision* 48(5): 713–731.

Weick, K.E. 1969. *The Social Psychology of Organizing*. Reading, MA: Addison-Wesley.

Weick, K.E. 1979. *The Social Psychology of Organizing*, 2nd ed. Reading, MA: Addison-Wesley.

Weick, K.E. 1995. *Sensemaking in Organizations*. Beverly Hills, CA: Sage.

Weick, K.E. 2001. *Making Sense of the Organization*. Malden, MA: Blackwell.

Yoo, Y., R. Boland, and K. Lytinen. 2006. From Organization Design to Organization Designing. *Organization Science* 17: 215–229.

CHAPTER 6

Foundations of Holistic Organization Design

Abstract This chapter introduces the model of holistic organization design, which is made up of three components: the hypothesis of organization design-as-meaning, the epistemological background of non-representational thought and the normative triad of morality, collaboration and purpose. The first two components are discussed in this chapter, while the hypothesis of organization design-as-meaning is examined in Chapter 7. The epistemology of non-representational thought provides a number of tools for understanding organization design as it happens, through the daily actions of the organization's members. Aesthetics offers an alternative way of making meanings, which influences the way people interact, behave and understand in the organization. The aesthetics and ethics components are linked mainly by the notion of reflective practices (Dobson 2022), which is the result of an elaboration of MacIntyre's (After Virtue. Duckworth, London, 2007) virtue ethics framework. This provides the background for the normative triad of *morality*, *collaboration* and *purpose*, originally inspired by the managerial theory of organization put forward by Barnard (The Functions of the Executive. Harvard University Press, Cambridge, MA, 1938) The triad forms a recurrent system of causes and effects, which guides all organization designing activity in the organization. The relationship between organization design and the organization's stated purpose is very relevant not only because

R. Magalhães, *Designing Organizations for the Betterment of Society*,
https://doi.org/10.1007/978-3-031-64483-2_6

organization design can be an *enabler of* or *inhibitor to* the attainment of organizational purpose, but also because it acts as a *mirror* of organizational purpose.

Keywords Aesthetics · Ethics collaboration · Cooperation · Morality · Purpose · Organization design-as-meaning

The repositioning of organization design proposed in this book is based, first and foremost, on the principle of design-as-meaning from design theory (Krippendorff 2006). In applying this theory to organization design, we follow Kazmierczak's (2003) contention that the content of a design cannot be obtained from the artefact itself but needs to be sought from the meanings constructed by the receiver in her contact with a design. According to that author, meanings are created and owned by the receiver and without an understanding of the receiver's inferred meaning, the content and the effects of the artefact cannot be known. In organization studies, there are several scholars who espouse a similar position. For example, Cunliffe (2008) suggests that organizations ought to be conceived as "emerging relational and dialogic language communities", where organizational features are not entities as such, but "shared meanings" and "shared ways of talking" (ibid.: 131).

The hypothesis of organization design-as-meaning, which is the development of a concept put forward by Magalhaes (2020), constitutes the first component of the new model of organization design (see Fig. 6.1). Taking the view that organization design(ing) can be defined as meanings as perceived by internal stakeholders as part of their regular processes of organizational sensemaking, this hypothesis is an ontological component. In attempting to answer the question "what is the nature of holistic organization design", it proposes that organization design can be considered at three levels of sensemaking: the level of intersubjective meanings, the level of organizational structures and the level of the design gestalt.

The second component of the model builds on non-representational tools, such as practice theory, sociomateriality and aesthetics, as tools that answer the epistemology question: "what theoretical approach should we use to study organization design"? In opposition to the static view of organization design-as-structure, non-representational thought highlights organization design as it happens in its sociomateriality, through the daily

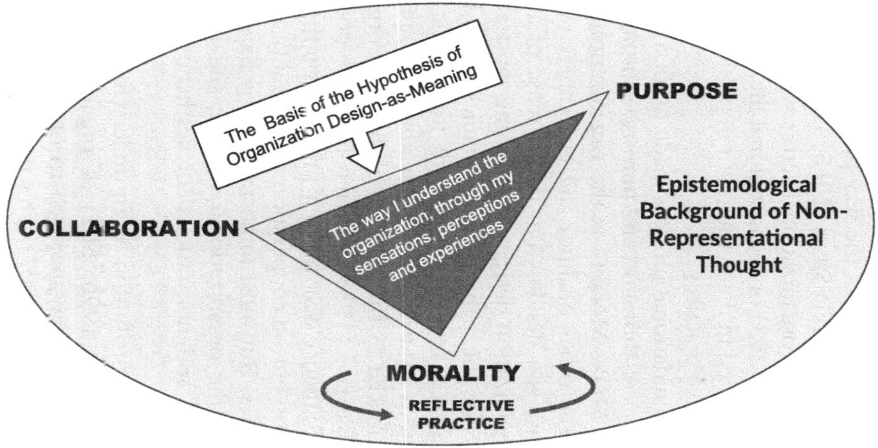

Fig. 6.1 Holistic organization design model

actions and experiences of the organization's members mediated by artefacts. The topics encompassed within the notion of non-representational thought are numerous and difficult to synthesize in some paragraphs or even a few pages. However, as far as holistic organization design is concerned, the key topics are morality, ethics and aesthetics. Taylor and Hansen (2005) explain that aesthetics offers an alternative way of making meanings, which influences the way people interact, behave and understand in organizations, while Strati (2015) suggests that aesthetic or sensible knowledge provides organizational actors with a "down-to-earth sensible experience" (ibid.: 253) of organizational life. The aesthetics and ethics components are linked in many ways, but in particular by Dobson's (2022) notion of reflective practices.

The model's third foundational block is made up of a triad of normative qualities—morality, collaboration and purpose—inspired by both the design discipline and MOS. Morality is the organizational quality that should rule over all the other qualities and encompass every aspect of design activity. Purpose is a desideratum in the sense of a "must-have" or something that organization design or designing must always lead to. Collaboration stands for the behavioural systemics behind every organizational activity and is a key reference point for holistic organization design(ing). However, as a starting point, our normative/pragmatic triad was also strongly influenced by the managerial theory of organization put forward by Chester Barnard (1938). Written from the point of view of the manager, Barnard's theory does not rely primarily on the properties of hierarchical organization but on cooperation and morality as foundational organizational properties. But most importantly, it is Barnard's focus on the need to consider "the organizational whole", and his emphasis on combining instrumental and non-rational or aesthetic elements that is truly groundbreaking.

Further to Barnard's contribution to an understanding of the "moral order" (Kogut and Zander 1996: 502) of organizations, our model borrows from an influential new approach to organizational morality—virtue ethics theory (MacIntyre 2007). This type of approach, which has been labelled by Dobson (2004) as "agent-based", highlights the role of the individual in the building up of ethical contexts and therefore provides an important contribution in explaining personal responsibility on the part of the organizational designer (i.e., the manager). Based on virtue ethics, Dobson (2022) suggests the notion of *reflective practice* as a means of maximizing the synergy between virtue ethics and organizational aesthetics.

The Epistemology of Non-representational Thought

Based on the generic account provided in Chapter 3, and considering the specifics of organization design(ing) discussed thus far, we submit that non-representational thought supports our conceptualization of holistic organization design in the following ways:

i. by emphasizing action-as-it-happens, rather than representations of organizational action;
ii. by stressing materiality and practice as foundations of organization and therefore as cornerstones of organization design(ing);
iii. by linking up practices, affect and meaning as contributors to organizational culture (Reckwitz 2012), considered as a sociomaterial manifestation of collective action;
iv. by giving prominence to morality, moral values and aesthetic judgement, and creating the possibility of connecting these to the development of individual and collective morality.

Starting with the first point, we posit that the main implication of considering organization design as action (i.e., designing) is that design becomes a *process of change*, which in turn means that *people* have a *central role* in the process. Through the daily actions of organizational members, lower-level or micro-organization designs change and many of such changes amount to new designs. Hence, organization designing happens by means of a mix of myriad planned and unplanned small design changes happening throughout the organization. From the point of view of the researcher, how can/should such changes be studied? A typical answer from organization studies would be to approach the problem by representing and analysing some independent variables, whereas an approach from a non-representational point of view would focus on analysing events as they happen. In their defence of the design discipline as the foundation for the study of organization design and following a non-representational point of view, Jelinek et al. (2008: 323) state:

> Above all, organization science as a design science engages with real-world interventions and results, not just abstractions from descriptive data.

As regards the second point, research into the materiality of social systems has long acknowledged that artefacts cannot be separated from the activity systems (Blackler 1993; Engeström and Blackler 2005) nor the practices (Gherardi 2016; Miettinen et al. 2009) where they are embedded. Monteiro and Nicolini (2015) explain that materials (e.g., objects, texts or spaces) are part of the way in which social processes and organizations are enacted, and that the material infrastructure through which work takes place enables and even orients interactions among organizational members. In the design discipline, Kimbell (2012) draws attention to the sociomaterial nature of practices, while Magalhaes (2020) submits that the notions of "design-as-practice" and "designing-as-practicing" can be applied to a situated conceptualization of organization design. And this links up to the third point.

Non-representational thought highlights not only practices, but also the meanings which make up the organization's design. The bond between practice and meaning is succinctly explained by Bille and Simonsen (2021: 6) through the lens of an embodied view of human cognition:

> meaning and significance are created *in* practice. The practically oriented body continuously weaves meaning throughout its life course, and its own capacities materialize through its interactions with others and with its environment.

Moreover, Giorgi et al. (2015) explain that certain practices act as meaning-making mechanisms and play a key role in the shaping of the organization's culture, by means of structuring interactions and guiding interpretation. Nicolini (2016) follows up this argument on the relationships between practices and culture, with the suggestion that when participants engage in their work routines, they speak a language, adopt behaviours and enter into relationships anchored on a "memory" developed by successive generations of practitioners working on the same routine. Such a memory is an intersubjective space that becomes intelligible within the pre-existing set of cultural-discursive conditions, which enable the unfolding of the practice and constrain what can be said and done. Thus, in considering the links between practices, meaning and culture and in acknowledging that practices are intrinsically affective (Reckwitz 2017), the discussion moves to the realm of aesthetic and ethical judgements. In other words, the non-representational concepts of practice, ethics and aesthetics are not incompatible with the concept of culture.

Hence, in addition to the emphasis on the here-and-now of designing activity and the focus on the real world of designing as being made up of organizational practices, the spotlight of non-representational approaches also shines on affect as a component of the cultural dimension of practice. On the other hand, in accordance with non-representational thought, *culture is essentially intersubjective* representing social phenomena as they are sensed, perceived and judged, and not just as symbolic representations. And given that practices are also affective, the sensing, perceiving and judging of social phenomena acquire ethical and aesthetic contours, which confirm designing has an inherently ethical and aesthetic activity. Thus, in adopting the principle of design as the creation of meaning as one of the intellectual bases for the theorizing of organization design, it must be acknowledged that the myriad designs created by the meanings of organizational artefacts create intersubjective spaces of "cultural-discursive" conditions.

Regarding the fourth and last point, Nicolini (2016) explains that practices guide practitioners' actions by helping them to make sense of emerging challenges associated with their daily routines, while a similar point can be surmised from MacIntyre's (2007) approach to ethics. Virtue ethics proposes that moral virtues develop in social contexts, while highlighting (work) practices as the locus for the development of virtues and character in individuals. This approach provides a model of organizational life, where members concern themselves with the questions of how and why they should make an effort towards the good of their community (Tsoukas 2018). The idea that practices create contexts where morality can flourish consolidates the link between the ethical dimension and the cultural conception of holistic organization designing.

However, as suggested earlier, holistic thinking in organizations has been defined by a managerial approach that allows non-rational or aesthetic consideration to blend with the rationality of regular analysis of organizational performance (Barnard 1938). Hence, for our holistic organization design model to be complete, an aesthetic element must be present, in addition to the ethical component. Such a combination of (non-representational) elements is provided by Dobson's (2022) suggestion that a phenomenological space where practitioners can ponder the possibilities of action within each novel situation, is required. This space of "aesthetic reflection" provides managers and other organizational members the opportunity to think about their activity without prejudices and away from the influence of the "corrupting power of the institution" (ibid.: 499). Dobson's theoretical framework, and especially his ideas about reflective practice as a fusion between aesthetics and virtue ethics, provides a significant contribution to our concept of holistic organization designing. To be examined in greater depth in the next section, under the heading of morality.

To conclude, non-representational thought provides crucial support to the ontology of organization design-as-meaning, based on the four points listed at the outset. Essentially, what this paradigm does is to change the epistemological foundations of organization design from rationalist positivism to a post-modern, situated and constructionist perspective that recognizes the materiality of organization as an artefact, as well as the sociomaterial, aesthetic and ethical nature of holistic organization design.

Morality, Cooperation and Purpose as the Pragmatic Normativity of Organization Design

First of all, let us clarify this section's heading. There is a belief among some academics that normativity and pragmatism are opposed qualities, and that anything pragmatic is devoid of moral values. However, according to writers like Hill and Troub (1995) or Ott (2017) this is not the case, and indeed normative and ethical considerations are inherent in pragmatism. Normativity refers to a designation of actions or outcomes that are deemed ethical, good or desirable, while pragmatism might be defined as a philosophical trend which holds that all reality has practical consequences and that the best way to understand reality is through the consideration of practical consequences. Not wishing to go into the philosophical debate, we will argue from the point of view of what is required from organization design as a topic of research and practice. This means that here we will argue from the point of view of the manager. Managers know what they need to make the organization function and to reach their proposed objectives, so managers need organization design theory to be pragmatic. But managers are also well aware that business success requires a degree of normativity. Hence, we submit that because most of what happens in the organization—functionally, behaviourally or in terms of business outcomes—is dependent upon the way the organization is designed, the foundations of the organization's design should be defined by both normativity and pragmatism.

Purpose

As suggested earlier, given that the organization's *purpose* contains the essential desiderata for the building up of the organization's edifice, purpose should rest at the base of the foundations of organization design, and include all the ingredients that make the edifice not only functional, but also ethical and beautiful. In management circles, the notion of organizational purpose is usually associated with the organization's mission, vision and business objectives; however, academic writers on business strategy, such as Nonaka and Takeuchi (2021), make a compelling case for business purpose to become more society-focused and conscious of the fact that maximizing shareholder value cannot be the only business objective. Along the same lines and joining a set of recommendations by the World Economic Forum, George et al. (2023: 1847) suggest that companies need to "produce profitable solutions to the problems of people and planet, and not to profit from producing problems for people or planet". In order for this to happen and for organizations to play their role in reversing global warming, decreasing the gap between the rich and the poor and dealing with pandemics that can paralyze economies, they need to embrace a *purpose* that is much more than a list of goals, but is anchored in a *sense of duty* and geared to the *betterment of society*.

A strong driver for the contemporary shift in corporate perception about the need to rethink purpose and include societal values and stakeholder entitlements is the new transparency provided by the internet, mobile phones and social media. Therefore, there is a new realization that companies can be rewarded or punished in line with their choices about the adoption of more socially responsible purposes (George et al. 2023). The same transparency also reveals how companies (and organizations in general) are converging with or diverging from their promises or stated purposes. With the help of technology, stakeholders are now better able to make judgements about their organization, by comparing their stated purposes with their internal and external conduct, deeds and actions.

Hence, organizational purpose should not be seen only as the outcome of a set of managerial intentions, but also needs to be considered from the point of view of the stakeholders, collectively, as well as individually. Conceivably, Barnard (1938) was the first management scholar to write about purpose, which he defines as the coordinating and unifying principle essential for any cooperative system to function. Crucially, Barnard emphasizes the relationship between the integrity of purpose and personal willingness to cooperate and explains that if the integrity of purpose is not maintained, people's willingness to cooperation breaks down. More recently, writing in the *Harvard Business Review*, Bartlett and Ghoshal (1994) propose that top management should not be limited to the traditional setting of strategy, but assume a more ambitious role in defining (or re-defining) organizational purpose. Accordingly, they recommend that purpose should: (i) embed corporate ambition, (ii) instil organizational values, (iii) give meaning to employees' work and importantly (iv) change its economic emphasis to a social one. Therefore, purpose should be seen as much more than a set of managerial plans, and something that is dependent on the perceptions and experiences of organizational members, and non-members.

Morality

The topic of morality in organization theory has been developed by many a management scholar; however, the school of thought which has made the strongest impression in later decades is stakeholder theory. Fittingly brought into existence by Freeman (1984) as part of the strategic management repertoire, stakeholder theory is especially attentive to the role of stakeholders in deciding the path and future development of their organizations, while generally mindful of the role of business and organizations in the betterment of society. Stakeholder theory proposes a new approach, whereby firms can enhance their performance by acting in a socially responsible manner towards all their stakeholders. Involving stakeholders in managerial decision-making will create more motivated employees, loyal customers, cooperative suppliers, improved reputation, as well as increasingly supportive communities (Harrison and Wicks 2013). Barney and Harrison (2020) suggest that stakeholder theory is not only about "describing human actors cooperatively engaged in value creation" but *is also* about encompassing "a worldview of business that reflects a higher state of consciousness about its short- and long-term role in and impact on society" (ibid.: 206).

Coordination (and/or Cooperation and/or Coordination)

A review of the literature by Castañer and Oliveira (2020) shows that the attitude, behaviours and outcome related and relatable to the notions of collaboration and cooperation seem to be similar, and one of the conclusions of the review is that if used with caution, the term "collaboration" can be used to signify the summation of the concepts of coordination and cooperation. Moreover, they submit that coordination can be defined as the joint determination of common goals, while cooperation can be taken to be the implementation of the agreed goals. Coordination is discussed by various authors, and links are established not only with cooperation and collaboration, but also with the concepts of purpose and morality. For example, collaboration is defined by Adler and Heckscher (2018) as "shared purpose", and by Bernacchio et al. (2022) as the "purposive coordination and cooperation, integrating heterogeneous inputs synergistically to create value" (ibid.: n/a). These authors take a step further by putting forward that collaboration is inherently ethical, and that the moral perspective is important because if management is viewed as driven by opportunistic, immoral and lacking moral legitimacy, people may refuse to cooperate; conversely, people are willing to cooperate when management is viewed as morally legitimate

MCP (Morality, Collaboration, Purpose) Triad

After this brief exposition of three foundational qualities of organization, originally put forward by Barnard (1938), we propose that they are closely related.

Starting with morality, MacIntyre's virtue ethics has been suggested by Bernacchio et al. (2022) as the theoretical underpinning of the moral order that lies behind the principles of collaboration among organization members, "comprising (…) excellence in collaborative activities" (ibid.: n/a). They clarify that the adjective "excellent" applies not only to excellence in products or services, but also to excellence in the life of the participant, while adding that:

> in today's context, excellence of both types will often involve sustainability, be it green(er) products that do not exacerbate climate change or a working life focused on devising more sustainable modes of production. (Bernacchio et al. 2022: n/a)

This citation highlights an important aspect of morality, i.e., the development of individual capabilities and of work contexts where individuals can pursue a flourishing life thereby contributing to the development of the organization and to the well-being of members and other stakeholders. Referring to the notion of virtue as excellence and implying that moral actions enable individuals to reach their full potential in all areas of human activity, Godfrey and Mahoney (2014) label such concern *developmental morality*. This concern is complementary to Barnard's emphasis on the organization's "higher purposes", and to the recognition of the instrumental value of organizations in producing communities that allow participants to develop and prosper.

Thus, it can be concluded that collaboration plays a fundamental role in sustaining moral agency, as well as contributing to human flourishing. To better engage in collaborative activities, organization members tend to adhere to standards of professional excellence, but over time, they develop virtuous dispositions, and begin to appreciate the intrinsic value of excellent work. Hence, we suggest that there is a strong a case to support the assumption that the triad morality, collaboration and purpose (MCP) constitutes an *ecological system* (see Fig. 6.2). Moore (2012: 310) reinforces this idea by placing purpose in the context of morality and collaboration, and highlighting the effect of such a triad on the formation of group identity. He states:

> an organization which has a *good purpose*, recruits and nurtures *virtuous employees*, pays fair and largely fixed salaries, encourages *participation* and self-governance, and has a trusting and trustworthy character will find encouraging group identity easier than one which tends not to have these features. (ibid.: 310, italics added)

A "good purpose" can be understood as a purpose, where the promises and expectations created by the organization are matched by actual realization. "Virtuous employees" are organizational members who understand the intrinsic value of excellent work, and the "participation" to be encouraged is the result of a cultural disposition towards collaboration

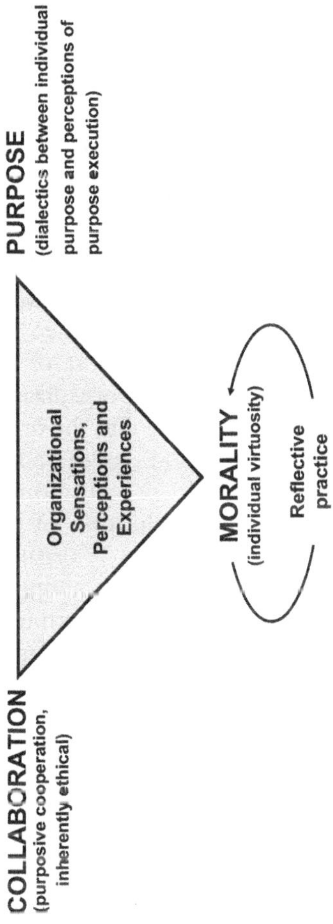

Fig. 6.2 The normative pragmatics of organization design

and cooperation. Hence, purpose can be defined as *an act of cooperation, which is dependent upon the (virtuous) contributions of individual organizational members*. Such articulation of purpose, as part of a system of causes and effects involving also morality and collaboration, is at the crux of our proposals for a repositioning of organization design. Thus, rather than business performance as the driver for organization design, we submit that the ecological system MCP should be seen as the *foundational driver* of a humanistic conception of organization design, as well as a prerequisite for good operational results.

The Interrelations Between the MCP Triad and Organization Design

Statements of organizational purpose are often *commendable* and *well-intentioned*, but the attrition caused by a variety of business, organizational and institutional forces make their realization systematically fall *short of target*. Over time, the disconnect between intention and realization of organizational purpose creates a host of problems not only within the organization but also between the organization and its external stakeholders. Behind all such problems, we find the organization's design.

The relationship between organization design and the organization's stated purpose is relevant because the organization's design works as an *enabler of* or an *inhibitor to* the realization of purpose. Organization design acts as an enabler of purpose if organizational members perceive that there is consistency between the announced intentionality of purpose and the organization's daily reality. Both internal and external stakeholders continually make judgements about various aspects of the organization's functioning, and judgements are based on perceptions and sensations. These are important and Glavas and Godwin (2013: 15) go as far as saying that "employees' perceptions of their company's social responsibility behaviours are more important than the reality within the organization". Hence, if perceptions of design/performance are positive, perceptions of purpose achievement will tend to follow suit.

On the other hand, organization design can be a major inhibitor of organizational purpose. One reason for this is that the *legacy* aspects of the organization's design, made up by the multitude of policies, systems and procedures that provide the organization with its operational infrastructure, can present a very real challenge. For reasons of internal politics and individuals' resistance to change, such legacies are often hard to reform, and they can become an obstacle to the implementation of a well-intentioned statement of organization's purpose. Another reason why organizational purpose can become a source of frustration and even conflict is the *meaning of purpose* at the individual level. As mentioned above, Bartlett and Ghoshal (1994) raise this issue and suggest that organizations need to associate purpose with giving meaning to employees' work, while Michaelson et al. (2014) also highlight individual purpose as having an impact on the design of jobs, interpersonal relationships, organizational cultures and even on moral issues in the organization (on this topic, see also Special Issue on Meaningful Work from the *Journal of Management Studies* 2019).

To be sure, organizational purpose is behind not only the moral development and human flourishing of organizational members, but also all other duties of the organization towards society and the environment. On the other hand, we have seen that purpose, alongside morality and collaboration, occupies a central position in organizational life and that the MCP triad can establish a normative foundation for organization design. Thus, organizations that are serious about the way they perform their duties to society and to the environment must *ensure that their designs are managed in accordance with the principles and values of their stated purposes*.

Dobson's Ethic-Aesthetic Theory of Business as a Development Tool for Organization Design

Based on the conceptual proximity between ethics and aesthetics, the virtue ethics approach is applied and extended by Dobson (2022) to business ethics to include an aesthetics perspective. He posits that in recent years there has been an increasing focus on the aesthetic nature of business and builds his argument by conceiving the firm as primarily aesthetic in the way it presents itself to the world. Hence, he proposes that the firm is not only an economic instrument, but also a construction of aesthetic sensations, where morality is postulated as something self-reflective. Thus, under the banner of reflective practice, virtue ethics and aesthetics merge and the notion of "practices" acquires a dimension of self-reflection. As discussed in Chapter 3, this allows the notion of practice in virtue ethics to free itself from its liaison with the economic interests of the firm and to remain the product of each individual's efforts to pursue a virtual life.

In our application of Dobson's (2007, 2010) theory to holistic organization designing, the "aesthetic ideal" is built by organizational members, individually and collectively, greatly influenced by the organization's managerial orientation. As discussed earlier, each organizational member constructs an image of his/her organization, based on his/her evaluation of the organization's execution of organizational purpose, vis-à-vis the promises made in the organization's public statements. Such aesthetic images are shared with other organizational members and in time, they form shared perceptions, conveying an image about the way the organization implements its announced purpose. Hence, it is always in the organization's interests to bridge the gaps that exist in the perceptions of intended and realized organizational purpose.

Indeed, this is the crux of Dobson's (2022) proposal, when he highlights the role of the firm in "nurturing reflective practices of aesthetic quality" (ibid.: 503), a proposal that might seem rather over-optimistic. Although such responsibilities have long been expected from firms, along with other exemplary practices, such as empowerment, participative leadership or positive discrimination, the sad reality is that organizations (including firms) simply do not deliver. However, if such responsibilities are framed within a more formal set of organizational arrangements, such as what is being proposed under holistic organization design(ing), quality reflective practices are more likely to flourish. The outcome of such reflection benefits the organization in creating a push from within for the organization to fare closer to the promises and expectations generated by its purpose statements.

In brief, virtue ethics and the notion of reflective practice help to define holistic organization designing in its task of steering the organization towards its purpose by ensuring that the principles and values behind organizational purpose are ever present in operational designs and percolate the entirety of the organization.

References

Adler, P.S., and C. Heckscher. 2018. Collaboration as an Organization Design for Shared Purpose. *Research in the Sociology of Organizations* 57: 81–111.

Barnard, C.I. 1938. *The Functions of the Executive*. Cambridge, MA: Harvard University Press.

Barney, J.B., and J.S. Harrison. 2020. Stakeholder Theory at the Crossroads. *Business & Society* 59 (2): 203–212.

Bartlett, C.A., and S. Ghoshal. 1994. Changing the Role of Top Management: Beyond Strategy to Purpose. *Harvard Business Review*, November–December.

Bernacchio, C., N.J. Foss, and S. Lindenberg. 2022. The Virtues of Joint Production: Ethical Foundations for Collaborative Organization. *Academy of Management Review*, published online: 8 September 2022. https://doi.org/10.5465/amr.2019.0389.

Bille, M., and K. Simonsen. 2021. Atmospheric Practices: On Affecting and Being Affected. *Space and Culture* 24 (2): 295–309.

Blackler, F. 1993. Knowledge and the Theory of Organizations: Organizations as Activity Systems and the Reframing of Management. *Journal of Management Studies* 30: 863–884.

Castañer, X., and N. Oliveira. 2020. Collaboration, Coordination, and Cooperation Among Organizations: Establishing the Distinctive Meanings of These Terms Through a Systematic Literature Review. *Journal of Management* 46 (6): 965–1001.

Cunliffe, A.L. 2008. Orientations to Social Constructionism: Relationally Responsive Social Constructionism and Its Implications for Knowledge and Learning. *Management Learning* 39 (2): 123–139.

Dobson, J. 2004. Applying Virtue Ethics to Business: The Agent-Based Approach. *EJBO—Electronic Journal of Business Ethics and Organization Studies* 9 (1). Retrieved from http://ejbo.jyu.fi.

Dobson, J. 2007. Aesthetics as a Foundation for Business Activity. *Journal of Business Ethics* 72: 41–46.

Dobson, J. 2010. Aesthetic Style as a Postructural Business Ethic. *Journal of Business Ethics* 93: 393–400.

Dobson, J. 2022. Virtue Ethics, Aesthetics, and Reflective Practices in Business. *Philosophy of Management* 21: 493–505.

Engeström, Y., and F. Blackler. 2005. On the Life of the Object. *Organization* 12 (3): 307–330.

Freeman, R.E. 1984. *Strategic Management: A Stakeholder Approach*. Boston: Pitman.

George, G., M.R. Haas, A.M. McGahan, S.J.D. Schillebeeckx, and P. Tracey. 2023. Purpose in the For-Profit Firm: A Review and Framework for Management Research. *Journal of Management* 49 (6): 1841–1869.

Gherardi, S. 2016. To Start Practice Theorizing Anew: The Contribution of the Concepts of *Agencement* and Formativeness. *Organization* 23 (5): 680–698.

Giorgi, S., C. Lockwood, and M.A. Glynn. 2015. The Many Faces of Culture: Making Sense of 30 Years of Research on Culture in Organization Studies. *The Academy of Management Annals* 9 (1). 1–54.

Glavas, A., and L.N. Godwin. 2013. Is the Perception of 'Goodness' Good Enough? Exploring the Relationship Between Perceived Corporate Social Responsibility and Employee Organizational Identification. *Journal of Business Ethics* 114: 15–27.

Godfrey, P.C., and J.T. Mahoney. 2014. The Functions of the Executive at 75: An Invitation to Reconsider a Timeless Classic. *Journal of Management Inquiry* 23 (4): 360–372.

Harrison, J.S., and A.C. Wicks. 2013. Stakeholder Theory, Value, and Firm Performance. *Business Ethics Quarterly* 23: 97–124.

Hill, L.E., and R.M. Troub. 1995. Pragmatism as a Normative Theory of Social Value and Economic Ethics. In *Institutional Economics and the Theory of Social Value: Essays in Honor of Marc R. Tool*, ed. C.M.A. Clark. Dordrecht: Springer.

Jelinek, M.„ A.G.L. Romme, and R.J. Boland. 2008. Introduction to the Special Issue Organization Studies as a Science for Design: Creating Collaborative Artifacts and Research. *Organization Studies* 29 (3): 317–329.

Journal of Management Studies. 2019. Special Issue: Meaningful Work: Prospects for the 21st Century. 56 (3): 481–724.

Kazmierczak, E.T. 2003. Design as Meaning Making: From Making Things to the Design of Thinking. *Design Issues* 19 (2): 45–59.

Kimbell, L. 2012. Rethinking Design Thinking: Part 2. *Design and Culture* 4 (2): 129–148.

Kogut, B. & Zander, U. 1996. "What Firms Do? Coordination, Identity, and Learning". *Organization Science* 7: 502–518.

Krippendorff, K. 2006. *The Semantic Turn: A New Foundation for Design*. Boca Raton, FL: Taylor and Francis.

MacIntyre, A. 2007. *After Virtue*, 3rd ed. London: Duckworth.

Magalhaes, R. 2020. *Designing Organization Design: A Human-Centred Approach*. Oxford: Oxford University Press.

Michaelson, C., M.G. Pratt, A.M. Grant, and C.P. Dunn. 2014. Meaningful Work: Connecting Business Ethics and Organization Studies. *Journal of Business Ethics* 121: 77–90.

Miettinen, R., D. Samra-Fredericks, and D. Yanow. 2009. Re-turn to Practice: An Introductory Essay. *Organization Studies* 30 (12): 1309–1327.

Monteiro, P., and D. Nicolini. 2015. Recovering Materiality in Institutional Work: Prizes as an Assemblage of Human and Material Entities. *Journal of Management Inquiry* 24 (1): 61–81.

Moore, G. 2012. The Virtue of Governance, the Governance of Virtue. *Business Ethics Quarterly* 22 (2): 293–318.

Nicolini, D. 2016. Is Small the Only Beautiful. Making Sense of Large Phenomena from a Practice-Based Perspective. In *The Nexus of Practices: Connections, Constellations, and Practitioners*, ed. S. Hui, E. Shove, and T. Schatzki. London: Routledge.

Nonaka, I., and H. Takeuchi. 2021. Humanizing Strategy. *Long Range Planning* 54 (4): 102070.

Ott, K. 2017. Normative Pragmatics: Approach, Promise, Outlook. In *Transcendental Arguments in Moral Theory*, ed. J.P. Brune, R. Stern, and M.H. Werner. Berlin: De Gruyter.

Reckwitz, A. 2012. Affective Spaces: A Praxeological Outlook. *Rethinking History* 16 (2): 241–258.

Reckwitz, A. 2017. Practices and Their Affects. In *The Nexus of Practices: Connections, Constellations, and Practitioners*, ed. S. Hui, E. Shove, and T. Schatzki, 114–125. London: Routledge.

Strati, A. 2015. Aesthetics and Design: An Epistemology of the Unseen. In *The Routledge Companion to Philosophy in Organization Studies*, ed. R. Mir, H. Willmott, and M. Greenwood, 251–259. London: Routledge.

Taylor, S.S., and H. Hansen. 2005. Finding Form: Looking at the Field of Organizational Aesthetics. *Journal of Management Studies* 42 (6): 1211–1231.

Tsoukas, H. 2018. Strategy and Virtue: Developing Strategy-as-Practice Through Virtue Ethics. *Strategic Organization* 16 (3): 323–351.

CHAPTER 7

The Hypothesis of Organization Design as Meaning—Sensemaking and Structuration

Abstract The hypothesis of organization design as meaning proposes organization design as a meaning-driven process of social construction. It is represented by a model with three parts (i) intersubjective sensemaking, (ii) structure and structuration and (iii) the organization design gestalt. The first two are described in this chapter, while the organization design gestalt is discussed in Chapter 8. The present chapter argues that in terms of its ontological origins, organization design is primarily anchored in the organization's *social form*, a pattern of interactions achieved at the level of intersubjective sensemaking. This means that in many ways what gives the organization its shape is the level of intersubjective sensemaking that the organization has achieved (i.e., its social form), which, in turn, has an effect on the way people interrelate. As organizations come to rely less and less on bureaucratic structures, social form is increasingly driven by intersubjectivity, with all the consequences that this trend implies, i.e., greater reliance on sensemaking and on embodied forms of cognition. This, in turn, has an impact on the evolution of the organization's structure, with improvisation becoming more prevalent and formalization becoming increasingly dependent upon quality of interaction. Hence, at the level of organizational structure, the chapter argues that organization design is largely shaped by the quality of interactions, a new concept that is explained as the level of "positivity" of experiences generated by interactions between participants, and subjectively judged as such.

R. Magalhães, *Designing Organizations for the Betterment of Society*,
https://doi.org/10.1007/978-3-031-64483-2_7

Keywords Formalization · Improvisation · Interaction · Interaction quality · Intersubjective · Organization design · Organizational sensemaking · Organization design gestalt · Social form · Structure · Structuration

> Why is sensemaking necessary? Because without it, it would be impossible to understand the 2456 corridor conversations, 342 meetings, 521 written documents, 5319 telephone calls, 413 hours spent on furniture moving and 12 conferences, as one story. (Czarniawska 2014: 40)

In this section and the next, various theoretical approaches, including sensemaking theory, social interactionism and organizational culture are brought together to explain the *ontology* of organization design. The model, shown in Fig. 7.1, is arranged in accordance with Weick's (1995) three levels of sensemaking—intersubjectivity, generic subjectivity and extra-subjectivity. The model of organization design as meaning aims at explaining the process of organization design as something that is perceived by organizational members on a daily basis. It ranges between *intersubjective sensemaking* at the individual level and the *organization design gestalt* at the collective level, with *structure and structuration* in-between.

The organization design gestalt is put forward as a cultural construction made up of collective values, perceptions and sensations embracing every aspect of the organization's design and exerting crucial influence on the experiences that people have of the organization. At the bottom end, intersubjective sensemaking marks the first contact people have with the artefacts or with other people through the artefacts. The hypothesis of design-as-meaning extends beyond cognitive processing and encompasses non-cognitive inputs based on emotional, affective and intuitive sensations.

The two ends of the axis (intersubjectivity and gestalt) come together in the middle to shape the organization's structure, generated by invisible processes of structuration, continually at work amid social groups. The organizational structure is made up of formal hierarchical rules as well as improvised action, shaped not only by processes of intersubjective sensemaking, but also by the quality of interactions between members. Figure 7.1 summarizes the model that has just been described, where

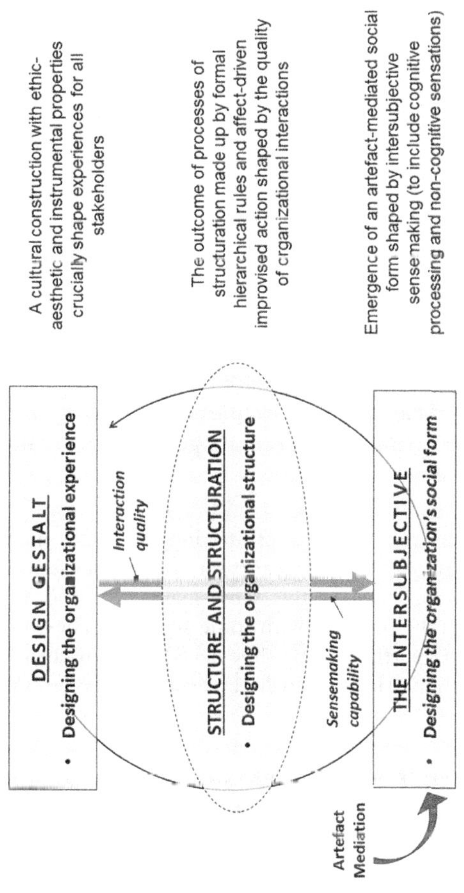

Fig. 7.1 The ontology of organization design-as-meaning

organization design produces three different outcomes: the design of social form at the level of intersubjectivity, the design of organizational structure at the mid-level and the design of organizational experiences at the level of the design gestalt. The detailed description of the model starts below, with the level of intersubjective sensemaking, followed by the level of structure and structuration. The level of organization design gestalt is described in the next chapter.

Intersubjective Sensemaking

In organization studies, the body of knowledge which appears as the natural complement of design-as-meaning in the design discipline is Weick's (1969, 1979, 1995) sensemaking theory. In an illustrious career lasting more than 50 years, Weick is credited with launching the twin concepts of organizing and sensemaking, where organizing is understood as the processes used by people to make sense of their world and reach a workable level of certainty by means of reducing equivocality. Sensemaking is about the structuring of unknown contexts or actions and assigning them with meaning, which amounts to saying that organizing is a permanent effort to make work manageable by creating sense and meaning. Weick explains:

> Organizations are in the business of making sense. If they attend to anything with consistency and regularity, it is their sense-making activities. Therefore, the outcome of this sense-making, flawed as it may be, nevertheless portrays the territory with some accuracy. These enacted environments are accurate partly because they have been consensually validated and partly because the territory is created by the map-maker. (Weick 1979: 250)

Through his work, Weick has demonstrated that the traditional perspective on organizing as a process whereby rational actors execute strategic plans to meet organizational goals is just too simplistic, because *acts of organizing are carried out by people and, as such, they cannot escape the limits of human understanding* (Weick et al. 2005). His focus is on flux, where the concept of organization as an entity is replaced by organization as a verb—organizing—while noting that *in the flow* of organizing, actors are always engaged in *interpreting* and *searching for meaning*. The results of such searching are translated into action (organizing) and the ensuing action is translated back into interpretation, in a recurring cycle (Taylor and Van Every 2000). This, we submit, is how organizations are designed.

Social Form as the Cornerstone for the Proposition of Organization Design-As-Meaning

Weick's approach to sensemaking was not conceived with organization design in mind; however, in his 1995 book, he makes a key contribution. Weick starts the discussion with the question "how does [organizing] action become coordinated in a world of multiple realities" (ibid.: 75) and in providing the answer, he contends that the key to organizing lies in the organization's social form, which he defines as

> a patterned activity developed and maintained through continuous communication activity during which participants evolve *equivalent understandings* around issues of common interest. (ibid.: 75, italics added)

According to Weick, one of the tasks of social form is to diminish the loss of understanding that occurs whenever there is a transition of meanings from the intersubjective mode to the generic subjective mode, two concepts used throughout his work. But before going into a more detailed discussion about these concepts, let us, for a moment, reflect upon the concept of "form" (as in "social form" or "organizational form"). First and foremost, "form" is a central concept in the definition of design and sometimes used interchangeably with "design". According to Nelson and Stolterman (2014), design is about the activities undertaken with the purpose of "giving real existence—*form*, structure and shape—to [an] idea" (ibid.: 1, italics added). This definition is supplemented by The Britannica Dictionary (2023), with the following entry:

> (form:) one of several or many different ways in which something is seen, experienced, or produced.

Thus, in addition to being the outcome of intentional designing activity (something produced), form (or design) is also the result of perception (something seen), as well as a consequence of human sensation (something experienced). This is an important set of distinctions, because it helps not only in defining organization design, but also in substantiating the connection between organization design and the meaning-based definition from human-centered design. As previously mentioned, design theoretician Klaus Krippendorff (2006: 42) considers construction and design to be "synonymous", which means that the belief held by social construction theorists that reality is made up by the negotiated meanings (Gergen, 1985) is shared by human-design scholars. Thus, in the context of a human-centered understanding of design, it can be asserted that organization design has its origins at Weick's intersubjective level of sensemaking (i.e., the "social form"), since designing, organizing and sensemaking are inescapably intermeshed. The meaning-based definition of design is also supported by the dictionary definition of "form", since meaning has to be present for a human to perceive or experience something.

Let us now go back to the distinction between intersubjectivity and generic subjectivity, and the role of social form as something that can diminish the loss of understanding in the transition between the two modes. Intersubjectivity refers to individual knowledge acquired through social interaction, i.e., sensemaking achieved through the merging or synthesizing of thoughts, feelings or intentions, which transition from the level of "I" to the level of "we". Generic subjectivity belongs to the realm of social structure, in the form of institutionally defined roles or scripts where human beings are no longer present. Frequent interpersonal communication about work reinforces the sharing of meanings through mutually reinforcing interpretations, which makes participation more mutually predictable. While intersubjectivity is seen as the source of improvisation and innovation arising from mutually reinforcing interpretations, generic subjectivity is encoded in interlocked routines, which provide the organizational structure with a degree of predictability.

Elaborating further on the notion of social form, Weick (1995) argues:

> Many current ideas about sensemaking assume vertical hierarchies (...) The routines, roles and expectations that allow for generic subjectivity and interchangeability seem to be giving way to intimacy, discretion, close proximity and smaller sized activities where people work primarily as collaborators rather than as experts (...) This suggests that intersubjective meanings—or perhaps some *new social form*—may be a new defining property of organization. (ibid.: 174–175, italics added)

Some important conclusions can be drawn from this excerpt. Firstly, it is implied that the current understanding of social form has been associated with vertical hierarchies and impersonal roles, which provide organizations with the benefits of generic subjectivity. In other words, by the mid-90s social form was still associated with the information-processing capacity provided by the organization's hierarchical structure. Secondly, Weick suggests that a form driven by intersubjectivity may be a new defining property of organizational form (i.e., design), not dependent on information-processing but on meanings generated by intimacy, close proximity and smaller-sized activities. Third, the excerpt highlights that the new type of social form allows people to work primarily as collaborators rather than functional experts, which reinforces the assumption that the ongoing trend towards boundaryless and virtual organizations (see Chapter 2). This necessarily implies that organization design theory needs to move from a paradigm based solely on analytical rationality to one where the rationality of traditional hierarchy is allowed to blend with non-cognitive, emotional and intuitive approaches.

The Movement of Social Form Between Intersubjectivity and Generic Subjectivity

In one of his most recent writings dedicated to organization design, Weick (2004) clarifies and expands some of his previous writings about social form. Firstly, he explicitly recognizes the overlap in meaning between design and sensemaking. He says, "designs have to be sensible themselves, and they have to help people make sense of the situations they face". Moreover, he describes design as a progression of steps of "compounded abstraction" that can be observed "when people try to make sense of the world" (ibid.: 41). Secondly, Weick suggests that managing the organization's design involves managing the *compounded abstraction sequence*, that is, the progression between sensations and perceptions rich in detail and achieved through the intersubjective mode, and the abstract representations found in the generic subjective mode of understanding/organizing, typically, more predictable but poor in detail.

He asserts that progression in the compounded abstraction sequence can be *monitored*, *contained* and *reversed* (ibid.: 41) and explains that as demands for coordination increase, "people begin to perceive one another in terms of roles and stereotypes" (ibid.: 42). In other words, as social complexity increases and the needs for transmission and coordination grow, organization designs become more structured, with participants relying less and less on the inconsistencies of interpersonal communication in the interest of greater efficiency. However, the movement away from intersubjectivity and towards greater generic subjectivity has costs in terms of "greater intellectual and emotional distance from the details picked up by direct perception" (ibid.: 42).

Lastly, in the above cited work Weick hints at another dimension of sensemaking which had not been developed in his prior writings, i.e., aesthetics. In clarifying what he means by direct perception (in the citation above), Weick defines it as "on-line automatic processing", as opposed to cognitive processing, which involves "stimulus-driven processing in order to take action" (ibid.: 42). Moreover, he explains "the details picked up by direct perception" as "primitives in both perception and design", or "zones of focus" that can also be described as "configurations or gestalts" (ibid.: 50). Such terminology resounds with the pre-cognitive nature of (organizational) aesthetics, which can also be explained as the experience or sensation of the holistic qualities of the people, processes or objects we encounter at every step of organizational life (Strati 1992, 1999). Thus, Weick (2004) not only recognizes aesthetic reality as part of organizational life, but also suggests that it needs to be combined with rational thinking, saying that "design can be seen as an ongoing effort to reconcile shared cognitions with idiosyncratic experiences" (ibid.: 50).

The More-Than-Cognitive Nature of Sensemaking

Historically, Weick's theorizing has emphasized language and discursive practices, that is, how written and spoken communication shape the creation of joint understandings (Sandberg and Tsoukas 2015). However, this cognitive pre-eminence has changed in the last few decades, with a number of authors demonstrating that sensemaking does include a raft of non-cognitive manifestations. Inspired by Varela et al.'s (1991) notion of enacted cognition and the idea that cognition is grounded in experiences gained through the body's sensorimotor capacities, Maitlis and Sonenshein (2010) open up the way for a crucial expansion of the sensemaking concept. They draw attention to the need to consider the role of emotions in sensemaking against the broader assumption that emotion is an embodied phenomenon; the authors also suggest a number of possibilities as occasions for sensemaking provided by the body, such as visceral sensations as cues and frames for sensemaking.

Further research by Maitlis et al. (2013) concluded that felt emotions can also influence the way individuals are open to noticing and perceiving cues and, more importantly, that sensemaking does depend on whether or not felt emotions are consistent with one's interpretation and action orientation. Cunliffe and Coupland (2012: 83) propose that sensemaking works "through sensory knowing and bodily sensations", while work by Heaphy (2017) has shown how participants actively generate, interpret and influence their own and others' emotions, thereby helping the organization to develop more collaborative relationships with clients. And in a study of how intuition develops into sense, Meziani and Cabantous (2020) theorize embodied sensemaking as a holistic, relational and transformative process, entailing a rich repertoire of bodily actions, including feeling, thinking, speaking and so on.

The results of these empirical studies and many more are reinforced and augmented by the research on embodied enactive cognition (Clark and Chalmers 1998; De Jaegher and Di Paolo 2007; Gallagher 2005). The work of Colombetti (2017a, b), for example, provides evidence for the premise that Weickian sensemaking is emotional and affective, in addition to being shaped by rational discourse. Rooted in research on basic living organisms, Colombetti (2017a) provides a useful comparison with improvised jazz music, a metaphor that has often been used in organization studies. She explains that the beautiful musical outcome is possible due to the coupling of two or more sensemaking systems (i.e., musicians), engaged in participatory sensemaking. Affectivity makes it possible for moods to be extended from one musician to the other(s) and for improvisation to ensue. As one musician improvises, the composite system made up by her brain, body and instrument produce sounds, which influence the mood (and therefore the sensemaking) of the other musicians, making them respond with improvisations of their own. Thus, one can say that it is in the act of playing and engaging in (participatory) sensemaking that improvised jazz music happens. This is relevant to the hypothesis of organization design-as-meaning, in the sense that it highlights the fact that, like sensemaking, designs are understood not only by means of rational information-processing mechanisms, but also through other forms of perception, such as emotions, intuition or gut-feeling.

The Role of Materiality

In his work, Weick does not establish an explicit relationship between sensemaking, organizing and organizational design. One of the reasons for this is that the materiality inherent in design(ing) is absent from the original formulations of the theory, and with the exception of a few glimpses scattered throughout his work, Weick does not provide much detail about the role materiality (Holt and Cornelissen 2014; Sandberg and Tsoukas 2015). That author does not go into the detail of how the materiality of artefacts plays a role in the bridging of designing and organizing. However, such a gap has been filled by a few empirical investigations, such as the work by Stigliani and Ravasi (2012), where it is claimed that the ways artefacts and practices enable individuals and groups to construct new understandings is largely missing from theories of collective sensemaking. Indeed, traditional understandings of sensemaking hold that the act of interpretation occurs when an abstract and pre-existing mental structure is connected to a cue, to produce meaning. The cue may take the form of a material stimulus, which could be an organizational artefact.

Stigliani and Ravasi's (2012) contribution shows that it is the manipulation of the material that supports the production of new abstract concepts and their infusion with meaning, that is, "by enabling the transition between (empty) abstract categories to concrete experiences, and then again from concrete to abstract" (ibid.: 1253). Additionally, these authors point out that unlike discourse, material artefacts are intrinsically durable and constitute a semi-permanent embodiment of experiences and ideas, which can facilitate the individual's prolonged retrospective reflection and the integration of these experiences and ideas into routine organizing. Inspired by Clark and Chalmers (1998) and the notion of extended cognition, Stigliani and Ravasi claim that the physicality of material artefacts extends the capacity of individuals and groups to process mental content. Artefacts support the storage and retrieval of mental content, enable the categorization of experience and facilitate the integration of mental structures. This contribution extends not only the notion of sensemaking, but also of organization design-as-meaning by showing how organizational artefacts can support or inhibit practices of collective collaborative through new interpretations and meanings.

Structure and Structuration

The definition of social form provided by Weick (1995) as a "patterned activity" developed by organizational participants and resulting from "equivalent understandings around issues of common interest" (ibid.: 75) feeds directly into the definition of organizational structure, under the hypothesis of organization design-as-meaning. The topics of structure and structuration are essential for an understanding of this new approach to organization design. According to contemporary social theory, (social) structures are produced by organizations as part of their regular daily activity, in recursive processes of structuration. According to Giddens (1984), social systems are composed of the "agency" and the "structure", the first representing the situated actions of the collective in its daily interactions, while the second stands for an invisible set of rules derived from previous interactions. In other words, agency creates the structure and structure governs the collective in its actions and interactions, in a mutually reinforcing way, and in permanent recursion. Giddens explains that structural properties (i.e., the structure) become institutionalized, making it possible for social (or organizational) practices to span space and time. In Weick's (1995) sensemaking theory, the same processes explain the notion of generic subjectivity.

In an oft-cited contribution, Ranson et al. (1980) explain the structuring of organizations as a process of generating and recreating *meanings*, embracing both the prescribed rules, positions and authority relations aimed at achieving a degree of predictability in organizational interactions (i.e., the *formal* structure) and the emergent configurations of interaction (i.e., the *informal* structure). In other words, in the light of structuration theory, organizational structure, which is a partial representation of the organization's design, is the outcome of the *mutual constitution of the formal and the informal parts of the structure*. For purposes of our discussion of the hypothesis of organization design-as-meaning, organizational structure should be understood as a perspective of the organization's social reality, which is continually in the making through mutual negotiation of meanings, and ever-changing relationships among actors.

Recent research by Soderstrom and Weber (2020) revisits this background and throws new light on the role(s) that structure may be expected to play in a reformed conception of organization design. Like Ranson et al. and many other writers on the topic, Soderstrom and Weber contend that both formal and informal structures *emerge* from processes of structuration, but they delve into the micro or interpersonal level and propose that the dynamics of interactions between organizational participants play a role in the processes of structuration. Indeed, the authors suggest that the emergence of structure depends on the ***quality of interactions***, with quality being defined as positive subjective experiences during interactions. This contribution represents an important step forward in the characterization of a situated perspective on organization design; however, before going into greater detail about this contribution, let us develop one of its key topics, i.e., social interactionism. This is also an important foundation of Weick's sensemaking theory and one of the supporting pillars of the hypothesis of organization design-as-meaning.

The Role of Social Interactionism

Although sensemaking has not been developed as part of social theory, it provides "micromechanisms that link macrostates across time" (Weick et al. 2005: 417) and explains how ***interaction*** generates social phenomena, such as organizational structures. Indeed, the meanings that are generated through sensemaking are also the basis upon which human interactions are built. Weick (1995) often mentions symbolic interactionist theory, "not so much because this is the unofficial theory of sensemaking but because the theory keeps in play a crucial set of elements including self, action, interaction, interpretation, meaning and joint action" (Weick 1995: 41).

According to the symbolic interactionist school of thought, individuals act based on the meanings that objects have for them, so that repeated, meaningful interactions among individuals come to be the defining basis of society (Blumer 1969). Meanings emerge from interactions between individuals, and they are continuously created and recreated through processes of interpretation (i.e., sensemaking) during social interactions. Just as in Weick's sensemaking, in Blumer's symbolic interactionism, meanings are intersubjective, constantly reinterpreted among individuals through their interactions. According to Blumer, traditional sociological thought treats human societies as composed of individuals who do not have selves, assuming human beings as mere organisms that respond to forces that play upon them, variously labelled as social system, social structure or institution. Such schools of thought ignore that human beings have idiosyncratic characteristics, which cannot simply be summed up as internalized social factors or psychological components, such as motives, attitudes or feelings.

Blumer's emphasis on individuals *who have selves* has inspired the "inhabited institutions" school of thought (Hallett and Hawbaker 2019; Hallett and Ventresca 2006), where the key message is that institutionalism needs to be "inhabited" and that focusing on interactions provides a means to examine action at the local level, while remaining in syntony with key aspects of institutional theory (Hallett and Ventresca 2006). Interactions take place continually across organizations, and they are shaped, but not completely determined by the institutional pressures that emanate from the macro institutional logics, such as bureaucracy. But the approach also focuses on the meanings generated by the interactions themselves, where macro-level logics and local-level meanings are negotiated, and new meanings are generated. These authors rehash Gouldner's (1954) famous study on bureaucracy, as exemplary of an "inhabited institutions" approach. In the study, the presumed efficiency of bureaucracy is debunked, with the argument that it needs to be examined not as an "ideal type" but in the way it actually operates. Gouldner identifies, for example, a "mock bureaucracy" as a social form involving an implicit negotiation between the workers and management, where bureaucratic rules are present but are systematically ignored. Thus, bureaucracy should be defined not by rules but by the *meanings emerging from routinized interactions*.

Hallett and Ventresca (2006: 223) assert that "interactions create (and recreate) social order, but they take place in contexts that enable, constrain, and shape them". This point is reinforced by Hallett and Hawbaker (2019) who explain that the institutional logics characterize the broader organizational environment shape but do not completely determine the form and content of interactions. Social interactions play a role in responding to institutional logics, as well as in shaping and refining them; they direct our focus of attention about what to attend to, as well as how to attend to tasks in the work environment. In this manner, interactions play a vital role in the establishment and maintenance of organizational practices, and through interactions institutional logics acquire local meanings.

Organizational Structure in Perpetual Movement Between Formalization and Improvisation

Subscribing to an interactionist perspective, Soderstrom and Weber (2020) suggest a scale of levels of structuration, ranging between formal and situational. At the "situational" level, the structure is entirely improvised, with the configurations of people, roles, norms, objects and places changing with every interaction, and outcomes not carried forward to other interactions. The intermediate stages—"provisional" and "informal"—relate to interactions, which are becoming increasingly routinized or formalized, involving prior interactions and agreements among the participants for the interactions to be continued. However, the routines are still discretionary in the sense that they are not included in formal organizational procedures. In the final stage—"formal"—interactions are not only standardized as part of procedures sanctioned by organizational authority, but they are also assigned to roles, which are not dependent on individuals. In Weick's (1995) terminology, this would correspond to the institutionalized level of generic subjectivity.

All the non-formal stages of Soderstrom and Weber's structuration processes display, although with different levels of intensity, characteristics of "improvised action", i.e., they all conform to the defining characteristics of improvisation—extemporaneity, novelty, intentionality, as well as referent role (Cunha et al. 2016). Thus, according to Soderstrom and Weber's framework, improvisation *is part of* an organization's processes of structuration; however, the cases investigated by these authors show a movement in the structures from the less formal to the more formal. This is probably due to the emphasis of this research project, on the emergence of structure in new business ventures, revolving around themes such as sustainability, CO_2 reduction or equal opportunity. The authors ask: "why do some new issues get enshrined in organizational structures, while others do not"? Underlying this question, there seems to be belief that in order to make an impact on society, emergent issues need to be formalized and encoded into structure, an assumption that would probably not be shared by Weick (2004).

As discussed earlier, Weick (2004) suggests that the movement from improvisation to formalization may not always be a positive development. He posits that in the movement towards greater formalization "details get lost, the concrete is replaced with the abstract, and design options get foreclosed" (ibid.: 41). Moreover, empirical research carried out by

Hadida et al. (2015) also suggests that structures can evolve from minor improvisation to structural improvisation, such as in the structures found in improvisational jazz. Hatch (1999) provides examples of this type of improvisation, when the entire jazz band develops a new theme, and the same idea arises again in future performances. Thus, if the result of improvisation re-occurs with some regularity, it can be said that ***improvisation itself can also lead to the emergence of an (informal) structure***. From this, it can be concluded that the notion of structuration of organizational structures can evolve in *both* directions (i.e., away or towards formal structure), depending on a variety of contingencies.

Thus, following the advice by Kamoche and Cunha (2001) and mindful of Weick's (2004: 41) observation about the management of organizational structures being "at the core of managing as designing", we posit that in the future formal organizational structures need to be conceptualized "minimally". This means, structures where the formal component is kept to a minimum and the informal (or situational) occupies the greater part, in permanent adjustment to fit the naturally occurring movements between formalization and improvisation. One important element to be taken into account when considering the oscillation between formalization and improvisation is the issue of ***interaction quality***.

Interaction Quality as a Shaper of Organizational Structure

In expounding upon the emergence of organizational structure and the movement towards formalization, Soderstrom and Weber (2020) talk about the possibility of structuration processes accelerating, halting, failing or even receding depending upon the ***quality of interactions***. They define interaction quality as "the extent to which interactions generate subjective experiences in participants during the interaction" (ibid.: 235) and emphasize that such quality derives from the *success* of the interaction. The terms successful and unsuccessful are used for describing the interaction experiences of participants, and as examples of successful experiences, the authors refer to events such as shared attention, increased emotional energy, understanding of the topic or intention to allocate time and effort to the issue at hand. Examples of unsuccessful interaction experiences are frustration or confusion about what the issue at hand, doubts about whether or not the issue is feasible, and ultimately disengagement from the issue. They conclude by saying that "the quality of situational interactions among organizational members is the engine behind the structuring of organizations" (ibid.: 226).

In Soderstrom and Weber's research, the assessment of interaction experiences (successful or unsuccessful) was carried out by means of the construct of *interaction trace*, explained as the outcome of previous interactions and recorded as changes in the states of participants (for example, "happier", "less confident" or "no longer willing"). The authors propose five different types of trace and argue that the notion of interaction trace is "the mechanisms that transform interaction activity into structure" (ibid.: 236). By focusing on the present and the past of interaction situations, it is possible to grasp the meanings and changes in meanings which create change in people's intersubjective understandings. This brings out temporality as a factor that should be considered in the study of organization design, a topic that has been broached by Yoo et al. (2006) in their study about design gestalt:

> Organization design then becomes a continuous shaping of the organization for its betterment (projecting to the future) in light of the concrete *trace of its past* (its here and now). (ibid.: 228, italics added)

Soderstrom and Weber's notions of interaction trace and interaction quality do not only raise the issue of *temporality*, but they also suggest that *emotionality* is a component of organization design, a suggestion supported by Hatch (1999) in her reflection about organizing as improvisational jazz. Relying on music terminology, Hatch (1999) firstly turns her attention to "tempo" as the rate or speed at which the music should be played and drawing a parallel with the management of organizational structure, she points out that tempo is important for coordination. The wrong tempo can lead to difficulties in coordination, therefore, managing tempo in organizations is part of the leader's role as the conductor of organizational orchestration. But, according to Hatch, organizational structures are also ambiguous and emotional, in the sense that improvisation in organizational decision-making often follows intuition and affect, rather than rational or intellectual considerations. She states:

> the feelings organization members have orient them to one another in particular ways, and these orientations are part of what constitutes an

organization's structure as patterns of interaction and relationship. (ibid.: 89)

A focus on organizational structure as patterns of interaction and relationship is essential for an understanding of the issue of minimal structures (Kamoche and Cunha, 2001), where the issues of emotionality and affect work in tandem with the topic of hierarchical organization. One of the best examples of such a design choice, is still the seminal article by Weick and Roberts (1993) on collective mind, which makes the point that it is possible to bring together the informality of emotions and affects, and the rationality of formal structure and organizational objectives. From their research on flight operations in aircraft carriers, these authors suggest that the "high reliability" nature of this work requires a structure based on *joint action*, not on rules and procedures. Joint action forms a social system, which is labelled "collective mind" and explained as a taken for granted "disposition", emerging from the dynamics of the group and affecting the behaviour of the group's members. The maintenance of "collective mind" depends on the quality of interactions and relationships (i.e., interrelating) among the group, which leads Weick and Roberts to conclude that heed and heedful actions constitute the interrelating that is behind the collective mind.

The recognition that heed, as a manifestation of emotion and affect, is a component of organizational structure, is also demonstrated by the research by Gherardi et al. (2019) on the sociomaterial traces of affect. These authors contend that traces of affect can be found in manifestations such as "the choice of words, the pitch of the voices, the crescendo in the verbal interactions, the mimicking of other (absent) voices, the broken language and the rhetorical figures of speech" (ibid.: 303). They claim that affect operates as a "shadow organizing" force, acting as a "conveyor belt", in terms of activity and movements within a situated practice keeping all its elements together. This work brings compelling evidence to the assumption that affect is behind the quality of interactions and relationships, which make up the organization's structure.

To conclude, the level of structure and structuration explains how organization design evolves from the intersubjective creation of meanings to the meanings emerging from social structure. The key takeaways from this sub-section are Firstly, the idea that structure is essentially a social construction and that, as such, structure has a *temporal* and an *emotional* dimension, both analysable by means of the study of interaction traces. Secondly, the *emotionality* component of organizational structure implies that the interactions between participants depend on emotions and affects (e.g., frustration, confusion or shared attention), which in turn create conditions for the type and quality of interactions and relationships. Thirdly, the *quality of interactions* plays a significant role in the oscillation between formalization and improvisation, which can become an important element in the management of the organization's structure. These three ideas pave the way for the top layer of the hypothesis of organization design-as-meaning—the design gestalt—where meanings crystalize and form cultures.

References

Blumer, H. 1969. *Symbolic Interactionism: Perspective and Method*. London: University of California Press.

The Britannica Dictionary. 2023. Entry for "Form". Retrieved on August 2023 from https://www.britannica.com/dictionary/form.

Clark, A., and D. Chalmers. 1998. The Extended Mind. *Analysis* 58 (1): 7–19.

Colombetti, G. 2017a. *The Feeling Body: Affective science Meets the Enactive Mind*. Cambridge, MA: MIT Press.

Colombetti, G. 2017b. Enactive Affectivity, Extended. *TOPOI: An International Review of Philosophy* 36 (3): 445–455.

Cunha, M.P.„ A.S. Miner, and E. Antonacopolou. 2016. Improvisation Processes in Organizations. In *The Sage Handbook of Process Organization Studies*, ed. A. Langley and H. Tsoukas. Los Angeles, CA: Sage.

Cunliffe, A., and C. Coupland. 2012. From Hero to Villain to Hero: Making Experience Sensible Through Embodied Narrative Sensemaking. *Human Relations* 65 (1): 63–88.

Czarniawska, B. 2014. *A Theory of Organizing*, 2nd ed. Cheltenham: Edward Elgar.

De Jaegher, H., and E. Di Paolo. 2007. Participatory Sense-Making: An Enactive Approach to Social Cognition. *Phenomenology and the Cognitive Sciences* 6: 485–507.

Gallagher, S. 2005. *How the Body Shapes the Mind*. Oxford and New York: Clarendon Press.

Gergen, K.J. 1985. The Social Constructionist Movement in Modern Psychology. *American Psychologist* 40 (3): 266–275.

Gherardi, S., A. Murgia, E. Bellè, F. Miele, and A. Carreri. 2019. Tracking the Sociomaterial Traces of Affect at the Crossroads of Affect and Practice Theories. *Qualitative Research in Organizations and Management* 14 (3): 295–316.

Giddens, A. 1984. *The Constitution of Society: Outline of the Theory of Structuration*. Cambridge: Polity Press.

Gouldner, A.W. 1954. *Patterns of Industrial Bureaucracy*. Glencoe, IL: Free Press.

Hadida, A.L., W. Tarvainen, and J. Rose. 2015. Organizational Improvisation: A Consolidating Review and Framework. *International Journal of Management Reviews* 17 (4): 437–459.

Hallett, T., and A. Hawbaker. 2019. Bringing Society Back in Again: The Importance of Social Interaction in an Inhabited Institutionalism. *Research in the Sociology of Organizations* 65B: 317–336.

Hallett, T., and M.J. Ventresca. 2006. Inhabited Institutions: Social Interactions and Organizational Forms in Gouldner's 'Patterns of Industrial Bureaucracy.' *Theory and Society* 35 (2): 213–236.

Hatch, M.J. 1999. Exploring the Empty Spaces of Organizing: How Improvisational Jazz Helps Redescribe Organizational Structure. *Organization Studies* 20 (1): 75–100.

Heaphy, E.D. 2017. 'Dancing on Hot Coals': How Emotion Work Facilitates Collective Sensemaking. *Academy of Management Journal* 60 (2): 642–670.

Holt, R., and J. Cornelissen. 2014. Sensemaking Revisited. *Management Learning* 45 (5): 525–539.

Kamoche, K., and M.P. Cunha. 2001. Minimal Structures: From Jazz Improvisation to Product Innovation. *Organization Studies* 22 (5): 733–764.

Krippendorff, K. 2006. *The Semantic Turn: A New Foundation for Design*. Boca Raton, FL: Taylor and Francis.

Maitlis, S., and S. Sonenshein. 2010. Sensemaking in Crisis and Change: Inspiration and Insights from Weick (1988). *Journal of Management Studies* 47: 551–580.

Maitlis, S., T.J. Vogus, and T.B. Lawrence. 2013. Sensemaking and Emotion in Organizations. *Organizational Psychology Review* 3 (3): 222–247.

Meziani, N., and L. Cabantous. 2020. Acting Intuition into Sense: How Film Crews Make Sense with Embodied Ways of Knowing. *Journal of Management Studies* 57: 1384–1419.

Nelson, H.G., and E. Stolterman. 2014. *The Design Way: Intentional Change in an Unpredictable World*. Cambridge, MA: MIT Press.

Ranson, S., B. Hinings, and R. Greenwood. 1980. The Structuring of Organizational Structures. *Administrative Science Quarterly* 25 (1): 1–17.

Sandberg, J., and H. Tsoukas. 2015. Making Sense of the Sensemaking Perspective: Its Constituents, Limitations, and Opportunities for Further Development. *Journal of Organization Behaviour* 36: S6–S32.

Soderstrom, S.B., and K. Weber. 2020. Organizational Structure from Interaction: Evidence from Corporate Sustainability Efforts. *Administrative Science Quarterly* 65 (1): 226–271.

Stigliani, I., and D. Ravasi. 2012. Organizing Thoughts and Connecting Brains: Material Practices and the Transition from Individual to Group-Level Prospective Sensemaking. *Academy of Management Journal* 55: 1232–1259.

Strati, A. 1992. Aesthetic Understanding of Organizational Life. *The Academy of Management Review* 17 (3): 568–581.

Strati, A. 1999. *Organization and Aesthetics*. London: Sage.

Taylor, J.R., and E.J. Van Every. 2000. *The Emergent Organization: Communication as Its Site and Surface*. Mahwah, NJ: Erlbaum.

Varela, F.J., E. Thompson, and E. Rosch. 1991. *The Embodied Mind*. Cambridge, MA: MIT Press.

Weick, K.E. 1969. *The Social Psychology of Organizing*. Reading, MA: Addison-Wesley.

Weick, K.E. 1979. *The Social Psychology of Organizing*, 2nd ed. Reading, MA: Addison-Wesley.

Weick, K.E. 1995. *Sensemaking in Organizations*. Beverly Hills, CA: Sage.

Weick, K.E. 2004. Rethinking Organization Design. In *Managing as Designing*, ed. R.J. Boland and F. Collopy. Stanford, CA: Stanford University Press.

Weick, K.E., and K.H. Roberts. 1993. Collective Mind in Organizations: Heedful Interrelating on Flight Decks. *Administrative Science Quarterly* 38: 357–381.

Weick, K.E., K.M. Sutcliffe, and D. Obstfeld. 2005. Organizing and the Process of Sensemaking. *Organization Science* 16 (4): 409–421.

Yoo, Y., R. Boland, and K. Lytinen. 2006. From Organization Design to Organization Designing. *Organization Science* 17: 215–229.

CHAPTER 8

The Hypothesis of Organization Design as Meaning—The Organization Design Gestalt

Abstract At the highest level of abstraction, organization design-as-meaning takes the form of a cultural construction. It is the site where the quality of interactions, as well as the effectiveness of the formal and informal organizational structures are achieved. A gestalt is perceptual by definition, but when applied to the social-material realm of organization design, the design gestalt acquires a cultural, meaning-making capacity, which is a reflection of and is reflected in all manifestations of the organization's design. The organization design gestalt is formed by cognitive and symbolic meanings, as well as non-cognitive sensations, such as emotion and affect. The concept of organizational experience is also central to our concept of the organization design gestalt. When stakeholders interact directly with artefacts or indirectly by means of interactions with other stakeholders, who are in one or another affected by organizational artefacts, they experience the organization. For example, when a customer talks to after-sales services, she has indirect interaction with an organizational artefact in the form of the computer application(s) and the host of company procedures that the after-sales employee needs to utilize in order to provide the service. Thus, the experience of the after-sales service is a consequence of the host of ethic-aesthetic judgements made by the customer in that particular interaction with the company. Hence, through the values and principles it encapsulates, and the behaviours it promotes, the organization design gestalt shapes organizational experiences.

R. Magalhães, *Designing Organizations for the Betterment of Society*,
https://doi.org/10.1007/978-3-031-64483-2_8

Keywords Aesthetics · Ethics · Cultural construction · Cognitive meanings · Symbolic meanings · Non-cognitive sensations · Emotion · Affect · Organization design gestalt · Organizational experience

According to Weick (1995), there is a third level of sensemaking—the extra-subjective—atop the intersubjective and the generic subjective. In the previous section, we discussed how design-as-meaning evolves from the meanings created at the individual level through intersubjective interactions between organizational members, and also how some meaning-making can be constrained by the rules emerging from processes of structuration. Structuration belongs to the realm of the social, and although originally sensemaking theory does not embrace this domain, we believe that social interaction is "a formative process in its own right" (Blumer 1969: 53) and that interactionist theory contributes to a better understanding of sensemaking at the level of structure. In this section we approach the third level of the model of organization design labelled the organization design gestalt, a level that influences all the other meaning-making and meaning-taking processes throughout the organization.

In the psychology of perceptual forms, the term gestalt is used to signify a pattern, a whole or a configuration. In certain cases, perceptual wholes are not determined by the perception of their individual elements, and the part-processes themselves are determined by the intrinsic nature of the whole (Wagemans 2018). This, we suggest, is the case with organization design. As a concept, gestalt contributes to the idea that at a certain level and in certain situations, the organization's design is seen as a whole, and its parts become irrelevant. An example of this is in the assessment of customers or potential customers of the organization's image or identity. Thus, like other artefacts judged by the perceived manifestations of their design, organizations also "display" their own design gestalt. Yoo et al. (2006: 227) define *design gestalt* as a "generative, form-giving capacity" and explain it as an organizational capability, which is the centre of the *entirety* of the organization's designing activity. They state:

> Designing products and designing organizations cannot be and *should not* be separated: instead, they both flow from the common set of capabilities that we call a "design gestalt". (ibid.: 228, italics added)

And they add:

> Organization design then becomes a *continuous shaping* of the organization for its *betterment* (projecting to the future) in light of the concrete *trace of its past* (its here and now) drawing on its design gestalt. (ibid.: 228, italics added)

Thus, the organization design gestalt is presented not only as a high-level concept pertaining to the perceptual realm and embracing all types of organizational artefacts, but also as a resource that organization designers "draw on" to bring about improvement and betterment to organizational processes. We find that these definitions of design gestalt can be expanded and made to play a larger role in organization design theory by linking them to the holistic level of organization design proposed earlier, and with the emphasis on the implications of design for the organization as a whole.

Thus, in developing the organization design gestalt as the capping of the hypothesis of design-as-meaning, we return to the teachings of Barnard (1938) and the need to adopt a mindset of "sensing of the organization as a whole and the total situation relevant to it" (ibid.: 235). However, in expounding the notion of organization design gestalt, we posit that Barnard's concept of "the whole" needs to be broken up into two interlinked components—organizational culture and organizational experience—underpinned by a single logic, the logic of ethics and aesthetics.

Organizational culture and the experience of the organization might be seen as two sides of the same coin; the former can be described as an *esprit de corps*, or the system of symbols and meanings, which creates cohesion and unity in social groups, while the latter refers to the organization's "aesthetic style" defined as the "sculpting" of the organization's "aesthetic chaos" (Dobson 2010: 393). The culture side provides a shared set of meanings associated with a host of ethic-aesthetic sensations and perceptions generated intersubjectively by the daily actions and interactions of organizational members. The experience side emerges either "live", here and now (as momentary feelings, emotions or affects) or retrieved and processed from prior memories, ideas or images. This *evolving combination of culture and experience defines the organization's design* as something that appears to internal and external stakeholders as a *gestalt*, understood as a "form", a "shape", a "pattern" or a "configuration" (of interactions, relationships and experiences).

The Organizational Design Gestalt as a Cultural Construction

In reflecting about the work of Weber and Foucault as originators of social theories for the study of organizations, Clegg (1994) outlines a number of reasons why we need a different conception of organization design. Firstly, he makes the point that we are not doomed by the discipline of bureaucracy, encroaching in almost every sphere of life, and explains that while Weber's model was indeed technically superior to any other form of administration, which has allowed societies to transition from pre-modernity to modernity, organizational bureaucracies are *still made up of people*. Thus, Clegg points out, the final direction of organizations will always depend on the moves people make in developing and deploying strategies for access to power and status, and not on any singular logic of rationality or efficiency, derived from certain organizational designs. Indeed, a Foucauldian perspective of organizational life provides a very different picture from that of Weber's bureaucracy. According to Foucault, power pervades the micro foundations of organizations and is present in everyday activity. Power does not have independent, objective existence, but should be explained instead as "the moving substrate of force relations which, by virtue of their inequality, constantly engender states of power" (Foucault 1980, cited by Introna 1997: 125).

Knowledge, according to Foucault, can only exist through relations of power, which means that power and knowledge are co-constitutive. Domains of knowledge are structured by power, meaning that in an organization the domain of knowledge, skills and know-how are entirely dependent upon the relations of power existing within that organization. A domain of knowledge includes a cultural element, in the sense that the people who share such a domain also share a set of meanings. Switching now to the realm of organization design, Clegg (1994) claims that this level of organizational analysis (i.e., the design level) is a form of cultural analysis, and against such a background, he posits an alternative view of organization design:

> Organization design is not some debased application of pure theory but the site of a practical cultural construction through conversation. To the extent that design involves more reflexivity towards its own and organizational others' meaning-practices, it may change meaning but cannot control it because it does not prescribe where the conversation may lead. (ibid.: 169–170)

Thus, Clegg suggests that the "design" component of organization design increases reflexivity towards members' own *meanings* and *practices*, which in turn means that certain types of organization design actively encourage change. Adding this to the first part of the citation, it can be concluded that organization design should be viewed as a cultural concern and a tool of organizational change. Moreover, Clegg emphasizes the relevance of cultural contexts in saying that because personal meanings cannot easily be scrutinized, contexts serve as interpretation mechanisms that stabilize the meanings of rules across people, time and space.

Clegg's welcome foray into organization design and its cultural nature finds echo in a remarkable paper by Claudio Ciborra (1996), where it is suggested that organization design (as a noun) should be conceived as a *virtual platform* embedding three types of interlinked components: material, cognitive and cultural. The material component is made up by the organization's practices; the cognitive element entails a collective cognitive scheme that governs interactions and relationships, and the cultural component comprises the organization's formative context. The formative context is a cultural construct, explained as a *social cognition* that transcends the individual and is embedded in material artefacts, procedures and in the relationships among organizational actors. Such a formulation helps us understand organization design as a mega-concept, made up of a variety of different components, covering all areas and all levels of the organization.

Design Culture

In the field of design studies, Julier (2006) defines "design culture" as "context-informed practice" (ibid.: 70), while Manzini (2016) explains it as the "meaningful context in which a new project is conceived and developed and in which new meanings are produced" (ibid.: 55). This author also talks about ***co-design*** as an activity that involves a variety of different actors, including professional designers, other kinds of experts, as well as final users, and he adds that often co-design involves a degree of tension and even conflict, a characterization that is very germane to organization design. In conclusion, Manzini suggests that a design culture will overcome the difficulties of co-design by facilitating ***dialogic conversation*** in the design process, a type of collaborative conversation where the involved actors are "willing and able to listen to each other, to change their minds, and to converge toward a common view" (ibid.: 58).

Thus, while "design culture" is mainly defined as the culture of the designers themselves and their client communities, design research also places significant emphasis on the importance of a design culture as something that will facilitate the emergence of contexts that can dissolve the problems caused by the different interests at play in every design process. Let us not forget that a significant part of the designing activity in organizations is "silent" and emergent (Gorb and Dumas 1987), which means that not only designers and managers, but also organizational members, as the end-users of designed artefacts, all have their own axes to grind. Thus, with so many people involved in designing activities, dialogical co-design through *collaboration* is an absolute must, and something that is part and parcel of an artefact-mediated ***design culture***. Thus, organization design as a cultural construction can play a crucial role in maintaining the integrity of the *spirit of the organization's design,* and as a space available to organization designers (i.e., the managers) to generate the conditions for cooperation and coordination among participants.

Artefact- and Practice-Mediated Culture

As previously discussed, Stigliani and Ravasi (2012) claim that the physicality of material artefacts extends the capacity of individuals and groups to process mental content, and also that material artefacts serve as external repositories of mental structures. This extends the notion of sensemaking by showing how the designing of material artefacts supports practices of collective collaboration in the construction of new interpretations and meanings. Collaborative practices imply interactions and relationships among organizational members, which in turn means that interaction and relationships are in one way or another ***mediated by artefacts***. This idea is developed by Monteiro and Nicolini (2015), in the suggestion that materials (e.g., objects and spaces) are part of the way in which social processes and organizations are enacted, highlighting the fact that human work always takes place through and amid a material infrastructure, which enables and even orients interactions between organizational members.

Indeed, as already mentioned, artefacts and materiality have a major influence on the organization's culture. Giorgi et al. (2015) explain that certain practices act as meaning-making mechanisms and play a key role in the shaping of an organization's culture, by means of structuring interactions and guiding interpretation. This is reinforced by Nicolini (2016), with the suggestion that interactions and relationships are anchored on a "memory" which is part and parcel of the "cultural-discursive" conditions that simultaneously enable and constrain the "unfolding of the practice" (ibid.: 104).

In the design discipline, Kimbell (2012) also draws attention to the role of practices and to the way that all designs are structured by objects, materials and practices. On the other hand, as it has already been suggested, practices act as meaning-making mechanisms with the capacity not only for structuring interaction, but also for anchoring down behaviour and providing a degree of stability (Giorgi et al. 2015). In other words, modifications in micro-level practices bring about shifts in shared meanings and "seemingly inconsequential changes to everyday practices could aggregate to bring about significant change to existing cultural logics" (ibid.: 31). This should now be seen in tandem with the views from Jelinek et al. (2008) about the need to consider organizational design not only as an aggregation of many organizational components but also the outcome of a two-way effect of the design on the designed and vice-versa. They affirm: "designing is about creating contexts and meanings that define components, as much as the other way around" (ibid.: 320). The thoughts from these scholars, supported by the already mentioned literature about materiality, artefacts and practices make it clear that the complexity of the consequences of organizational artefacts on the behaviour, the experience and the performance of the organization, indicates that culture (or the extra-subjective) is an appropriate level at which to conceptualize organization design.

Concluding: The Organization Design Gestalt as an Extended Cultural Construction Embracing Artefact Mediation, Image and Identity

To end this section, we posit that Clegg's proposal of organization design as a practical cultural construction and Ciborra's notion of organization design as a virtual platform supported by a formative context, along with the perspectives on design culture from theoreticians Julier and Manzini, aptly supplement Yoo et al.'s (2006) notion of design gestalt as capstone of our organization design model. Fused into a single concept, the *design gestalt* and the organization design as a social construction (hereafter "the organization design gestalt") can be understood as a virtual organizational capability that allows organizations to combine "ideas, values, resources, tools, and people into ensembles that can create and project remarkable artifacts" (Yoo et al. 2006: 228). And continuing to lean on Yoo and colleagues and their assertion that the designing organizations cannot be separated from the designing of products, this means that in order to encompass the entirety of the organization, the organization design gestalt needs to be specified very broadly and include all the internal and external aspects of the organization's activity.

This requires an equally broad perspective on organizational culture, a requirement that can be found in Hatch's (1993) little known but particularly apt approach. That author defines culture as a phenomenon that is "constituted by continuous cycles of action and meaning-making shadowed by cycles of image and identity formation" (ibid.: 686). According to the work of this author and colleagues, external features of organization, such as identity and image, should also be considered as part of the organization's culture (Hatch and Schultz 1997, 2002). This is relevant to organization design, in the sense that changes in artefacts and artefact mediation will undoubtedly bring about changes in the organization's *meaning-making* capabilities and therefore in its cultural contexts. Thus, it is suggested that the organization design gestalt and the organization's culture overlap to a large extent, in terms of the type of phenomenon that these concepts represent. However, the design gestalt highlights some features of the organization's culture that were, which have not been considered relevant enough to be theorized separately.

Pursuing Jelinek et al.'s (2008) assertion that "the kind of artifact created in our minds and enacted in our behaviour affects the process and outcomes of our efforts to create organizational entities" (ibid.: 321), we submit that the way we intentionally create artefacts will inevitably affect the organization's culture through the effects of organizational artefacts on interactions, relationships and contexts of meaning. Indeed, it can be assumed that perceptions about the organization and its products and services, as well as all other artefacts used internally or externally carry values, and attract judgements, such as good, bad, fair, beautiful, respectful or inconsiderate. This means that when people engage with the organization, either as external entities or internal stakeholders, they form ethic-aesthetic judgements based on their *experiences*. Such ethic-aesthetic component of the invisible culture that scaffolds the organization is the contribution of the organization design gestalt.

The Organizational Design Gestalt as a Shaper of Organizational Experience

In interpreting the concept of "cultural" as the result of symbolic as well as embodied meanings acquired by means of the sensory lenses of ethics and aesthetics, the notion of cultural construction is taken to the realm of non-representational epistemology and becomes also "experiential". Strati (2015) explains that organizational experience is "designed", and that organizational interactions are concrete relationships with a *pathos* made up of the emotions and the materiality of organizational experience. A great deal of organizational life includes organizational experiences; however, this is usually not recognized either by practising managers or academic researchers because it eludes the cognitive level of intelligence. Such a knowledge gap, which affects our understanding of organizations and their management, has been highlighted by social science scholars for decades:

> Aesthetic experiences, which are often considered subjective and hence inessential by social scientists, thus actually may be one of the essential ways we learn to become *objective*, in the sense of coming to recognize the pervasive qualities of the environment in their own terms. (Csikszentmihalyi and Rochberg-Halton 1981, cited by Gagliardi 2006: 713)

Fortunately, there are increasing signs of a turn in MOS research in favour of non rational, pre-cognitive or aesthetic elements of organizational life as research components, in addition to or instead of many of the taken-for-granted precepts from mainstream MOS. Organizational aesthetics emphasizes the fact that workplace interactions are corporealities that belong to individuals, groups and collectives, not mental constructs, nor semiotic concepts (Strati 2015). On the other hand, Creed et al. (2020) suggest that the aesthetic mode enables people to *experience organization* through the viewpoints of both personal and institutional aesthetics. Our personal aesthetic develops over our lifetime as we learn how to respond to various sensations and not just when we are exposed to an out-of-the-ordinary experience of beauty. It guides our daily life on mundane activities, allowing us to see, hear, taste, smell and feel "with meaning" (Taylor 2018). Learned from our history of being in the world, we have many different aesthetics available to us, reflecting the many contacts we have with many different social groupings, in different social contexts. Hence, the aesthetics of individual organizational members, which is the main input for organizational experience, is the result of the member's personal aesthetics and her/his internalization of the organization's aesthetic codes (Creed et al. 2020).

Thus, organizational experience can be understood as the outcome of the host of cultural judgements that organizational members, as well as external stakeholders, make about the multitude of internal and external features of the organization's design (Ramírez 1996; Wasserman and Frenkel 2011). Ramírez (1996) goes far as suggesting that we may interpret "organizational form" (i.e., the organization's design) as the way we *experience* organizations, as well as the way we convey our experiences of them. He describes organizational design as the "actions and interactions which constitute organizations for different stakeholders" (ibid.: 234). Organizational experiences can take many shapes and forms, some internal, such as the experience of policies, procedures, systems or internal communications, and some external, such as the experience of the organization's products, brands, logos, buildings or corporate colours.

From this, we suggest that the organization design gestalt as organizational experience might be explained as the way people are able to distinguish what is beautiful or shocking, ethical or unethical about their experience of/with the organization. However, experiences for internal and external stakeholders are quite different. External stakeholders rely mostly on their prior knowledge of the organization's image and identity, while internal stakeholders have the benefit of the organization-wide sharing of aesthetic experiences, which includes the sharing of individual members' values and sensibilities (Shrivastava et al. 2017). Having the ability to understand such differences is an essential organizational competence that hitherto has not been considered particularly relevant; however, such competence is now being proposed as part of the portfolio of competencies of the holistic organization designer.

Summing Up the Complete Model of Organization Design-As-Meaning

The model of organization design-as-meaning, shown in Fig. 7.1, is intended to answer the question "what is organization design", under the assumption that organization design can be defined as a perception or set of meanings for internal and external stakeholders. The hypothesis of organization design-as-meaning encompasses both layers of organization design, which for purposes of design management, we have split into a lower layer of operational concerns and an upper layer of holistic organization designing. For purposes of ontological description and inspired by the conceptual proximity between human-centred design and sensemaking theory, the model proposes organization design as a meaning-driven process of social construction operating at three levels: the intersubjective, which relies on sensemaking at the intersubjective level; organizational structure, which relies on symbolic interactionism and mechanisms of social structuration; and the organization design gestalt, conceptualized as a cultural construction, shaping contexts of meaning that carry principles and values about the organization's design and serve as the significance platform for organizational experiences.

The principles and values of the design gestalt, which should also govern the design and operation of organizational artefacts percolate the interactions and relationships of organization members at all levels. Hence, through the cultural frame, artefacts, interactions and relationships play a crucial role in the shaping of organizational experiences for all stakeholders (internal and external). Managerial postures on morality, social responsibility, environmental priorities, sustainability, as well as other social and environmental concerns will be reflected in the organization design gestalt and through it, they will shape the entirety of the organization. Thus, the linkages between the upper and lower levels of organization design emerge as very relevant and together they determine the design, but before we look at these, let us briefly review the key concepts of organization design-as-meaning.

Social Form and Organizational Structure

We have argued that in terms of its ontological origins, organization design is primarily anchored in the organization's *social form*, a pattern of interactions achieved at the level of intersubjective sensemaking. This means that in many ways what gives the organization its shape (i.e., its design) is the level of intersubjective sensemaking that the organization has achieved (i.e., its social form). Traditionally, the social form was seen as something dependent upon the information-processing capacity provided by the organization's hierarchical structure, but as organizations came to rely less and less on bureaucratic structures, social form is increasingly driven by intersubjectivity, with all the consequences that this implies. One of the consequences is a greater reliance on sensemaking, interpretation and meaning-making, based on interpersonal proximity and ways of knowledge acquisition, which allow for sensory or non-rational inputs.

This, in turn, has an impact on the evolution of the organization's structure, with informality and improvisation becoming ever more prevalent and increasingly dependent upon the quality of interaction. Hence, at the level of organizational structure, organization design is largely shaped by the quality of interactions, a new concept that has been explained as the level of "positivity" of experiences generated by interactions between participants, as subjectively judged by the participants. More positive experiences tend to lead towards greater permanence in interactions and therefore greater propensity towards formalization of structure. In fact, organizational structure can be seen as a dynamic form resulting from the perpetual push-and-pull between formalization and improvisation.

Design Gestalt and Organizational Experience

At the highest level of abstraction, organization design-as-meaning takes the form of a cultural construction, woven into the organization's culture, and identifiable as the organization design gestalt. A gestalt is perceptual by definition and when applied to the social-material realm of organization design, the design gestalt acquires a cultural, meaning-making capacity, which is reflected in all manifestations of organizational life. The organization design gestalt is also behind the quality of interactions. In other words, when members interact while engaged in their daily routines, their interactions reflect, firstly, the way they make sense of their tasks and secondly, the beliefs and values that have been instilled into the culture of the design gestalt. This affects the quality of the interaction, but there is another phenomenon, which also affects interaction quality, i.e., *organizational experience*.

The concept of organizational experience is equally central to our concept of the organization design gestalt. When stakeholders interact directly with artefacts or indirectly by means of interactions with other stakeholders, who are in one or another affected by organizational artefacts, they experience the organization. For example, when a customer talks to after-sales services, she has indirect interaction with an organizational artefact in the form of the computer application(s) and the host of company procedures that the after-sales employee needs to utilize in order to provide the service. Thus, the experience of the after-sales service is a consequence of the host of ethic-aesthetic judgements made by the customer in that particular interaction with the company. Hence, through the values and principles it encapsulates, and the behaviours it promotes, the organization design gestalt shapes organizational experiences. By the same token, the experience of artefacts such as the organization's policies, procedures, systems or internal communications, as well as the experience to the organization's products, brands, logos, buildings or corporate colours go through the filters of the organization design gestalt.

Artefact Mediation

Artefact creation, maintenance and operation are pivotal concerns of our approach to organization design, which means that artefact mediation is also a key concept. By mediation we mean the positioning of the artefact between the person and the task. In other words, for organizational members to carry out their tasks, they use artefacts, which means that the way the task is accomplished depends on the artefact. But mediation is also important because the way that artefacts are designed will affect the way people work, interact and create relationships, which in turn will affect the organization's design. The model of organization design-as-meaning assumes the influence of artefact mediation at the level of each organizational member, but it also acknowledges the influence of artefact mediation at the level of structure and at the level of the organization design gestalt.

Intersubjective sensemaking is the level where the consequences of artefact mediation are felt individually, while at the level of organizational structure artefact mediation is reflected in the interactions between members, while going about their tasks, or routines. At the level of the organization design gestalt, artefact mediation has a much wider role, playing a part in every interaction between internal stakeholders and the organization (not necessarily as part of the formal structure), as well as in the interactions between external stakeholders and the organization.

Linking the Holistic and the Operational/Technical/Local Layers

Having concluded the synthesis of organization-design-as-meaning, we are now ready to propose how the two levels of organization design are linked. Figure 8.1 conveys the gist of the argument.

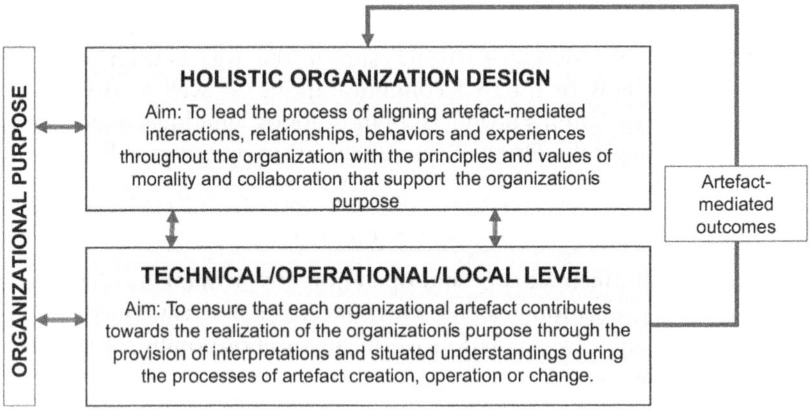

Fig. 8.1 The double-layered organization design framework

The Operational/Technical/Local Layer

Influenced by Krippendorff's (2006) view of design as the creation of meaning, Jelinek et al. (2008) suggest that if organization research is to become a design science, it must acknowledge that "artifacts are created in view of the meanings given to them; these meanings can be very diverse and ambiguous (e.g., products, management tools, networks, projects, discourses) and tend to interact and feed-back on each other" (ibid.: 324). The authors explain that organizational artefacts are essentially unstable because they are given new *meaning* through *interaction*, which means that they are continually recreated over the course of their existence. The process of creation of organizational artefacts is entirely serendipitous in the sense that the assumptions that were made at the start of the process keep changing in the interplay of ideas and constraints, and organizations always end up with artefacts that are different from what was originally intended. Such serendipity, they claim, imperils "any theoretical architecture based on assumed (but fictional) stability" (ibid.: 320).

Thus, given the variety of purposes, types and levels of organizational artefacts (see Chapter 4), it is not feasible to ponder any universal rules for the design and construction of the entire infrastructure of artefacts. However, it is possible to consider the overall principles (and values) that can guide the meanings (interpretations, expectations, roles and relationships) of both designers and users of the artefacts (Jelinek et al., 2008) The emphasis on the meaning of artefacts resonates with Weick's (2001) teachings about improvised organization design and the suggestion that the purpose of design is to *facilitate interpretation* rather than to facilitate decision-making, and that the organization's *effectiveness* is determined by its ability to interpret, not its ability to make decisions (see Table 2.1).

The ability to interpret should be understood in its broad sense, to include not only the macro issues that affect the organization's competitiveness, but also the micro issues emerging from the implementation of organizational artefacts. Kimbell (2011) characterizes designers as "a diverse group of people (...) involved in constructing and interpreting the meaning of a design" (ibid.: 43) going on to describe the process of designing as being "shaped by a situated understanding of the issue at hand" (ibid.: 42). This description fits our conception of the organization designer's role at the *operational/technical level*, where the emphasis is on *providing interpretation, clarification and situated understandings of/about organizational artefacts* throughout the stages of construction, implementation, deployment and use.

The Holistic Level

Considering that the creation and implementation of artefacts at the local level changes meanings, it can be assumed that the way we create artefacts affects the contexts of meaning *across the entire organization* through the mediation of artefacts on interactions and relationships. Thus, we suggest that *artefact mediation* has an important role in the linkage between the two levels of organization design, as shown in Fig. 8.1. An understanding of the upper level of organization design as essentially perceptual, sensory and cultural is also relevant because it allows us to establish a relationship between organization design and organization experience. A design culture refers to the principles and values that are customarily followed in all design activities, whereas organization experience refers to the way organizational artefacts, such as policies, procedures, systems, internal communications, products, brands, logos or buildings are sensed and judged by internal and external stakeholders. This, in turn, implies that at the holistic level organization design assumes the true sense of the expression "organizational design", that is, a set of *perception of the organization*, either of the whole organization or of some of its parts.

The figure also highlights the types of roles that are required from the organization designer. At the upper level, the role is aimed at leading collaboration and coordination in a climate of morality through self-reflection. The final purpose of holistic organization designing is to ensure that the principles and values behind the organization's purpose percolate the *organization as an artefact*. This is achieved by means of a (design) culture that shapes interactions, relationships and experiences within the organization and between the organization and its external stakeholders. The activity at the holistic level will obviously shape, enhance or constrain activity at the operational/technical level, where the role of the organization designer is to provide interpretations and situated understandings about definitions, meanings and approaches in the process of artefact creation, all in line with the principles and values behind the organization's purpose.

References

Barnard, C.I. 1938. *The Functions of the Executive*. Cambridge, MA: Harvard University Press.

Blumer, H. 1969. *Symbolic Interactionism: Perspective and Method*. London: University of California Press.

Ciborra, C.U. 1996. The Platform Organization: Recombining Strategies, Structures and Surprises. *Organization Science* 7: 103–118.

Ciborra, C.U., and G.F. Lanzara. 1990. Designing Dynamic Artifacts: Computer Systems as Formative Contexts. In *Symbols and Artifacts: Views of the Corporate Landscape*, ed. P. Gagliardi. New York: Aldine DeGruyter.

Clegg, S. 1994. Weber and Foucault: Social Theory for the Study of Organizations. *Organization* 1 (1): 149–178.

Creed, W.E.D., S.S. Taylor, and B.A. Hudson. 2020. Institutional Aesthetics: Embodied Ways of Encountering, Evaluating, and Enacting Institutions. *Organization Studies* 41 (3): 415–435.

Csikszentmihalyi, M., and E. Rochberg-Halton. 1981. *The Meaning of Things*. Cambridge: Cambridge University Press.

Dobson, J. 2010. Aesthetic Style as a Postructural Business Ethic. *Journal of Business Ethics* 93: 393–400.

Foucault, M. 1980. *The History of Sexuality*, vol. 1. New York: Vintage Books.

Gagliardi, P. 2006. Exploring the Aesthetic Side of Organizational Life. In *The Sage Handbook of Organizations Studies*, ed. S.R. Clegg, C. Hardy, T.B. Lawrence, and W.R. Nord. London: Sage.

Giorgi, S., Lockwood, C., & Glynn, M. A. 2015. "The Many Faces of Culture: making sense of 30 years of research on culture in organization studies". *The Academy of Management Annals* (9) 1: 1–54.

Gorb, P., & Dumas, A. 1987. "Silent Design". *Design Studies* (8) 3: 150–156.

Hatch, M. J. 1993. "The Dynamics of Organizational Culture". *Academy of Management Review* 18: 657–693.

Hatch, M. J., & Schultz, M. 1997. "Relations between organizational culture, identity and image". *European Journal of Marketing* 31 (5/6): 356–365.

Introna, L.D. 1997. *Management, Information and Power: A Narrative of the Involved Manager*. London: Macmillan.

Jelinek, M., A.G.L. Romme, and R.J. Boland. 2008. Introduction to the Special Issue Organization Studies as a Science for Design: Creating Collaborative Artifacts and Research. *Organization Studies* 29 (3): 317–329.

Julier, G. 2006. From Visual Culture to Design Culture. *Design Issues* 22 (1): 64–76.

Kimbell, L. 2011. Designing for Service as One Way of Designing Services. *International Journal of Design* 5 (2): 41–52.

Kimbell, L. 2012. "Rethinking Design Thinking: part 2". *Design and Culture* 4 (2): 129–148

Kimberly, J.R. 1984. The Anatomy of Organizational Design. *Journal of Management* 10 (1): 109–126.

Krippendorff, K. 2006. *The Semantic Turn: A New Foundation for Design*. Boca Raton, FL: Taylor and Francis.

Manzini, E. 2016. Design Culture and Dialogic Design. *Design Issues* 32 (1): 52–59.

Monteiro, P., & Nicolini, D. 2015. "Recovering Materiality in Institutional Work: prizes as an assemblage of human and material entities". *Journal of Management Inquiry* 24 (1): 61–81.

Nicolini, D. 2016. "Is Small the Only Beautiful. Making Sense of Large Phenomena from a Practice-Based Perspective". In S. Hui, E. Shove and T. Schatzki (eds), *The Nexus of Practices: connections, constellations, and practitioners*. London: Routledge

Ramírez, R. 1996. Wrapping Form and Organizational Beauty. *Organization* 3 (2): 233–242.

Shrivastava, P., G. Schumacher, D.M. Wasieleski, and M. Tasic. 2017. Aesthetic Rationality in Organizations: Toward Developing a Sensitivity for Sustainability. *The Journal of Applied Behavioural Science* 53 (3): 369–411.

Stigliani, I. & Ravasi, D. 2012. "Organizing Thoughts and Connecting Brains: material practices and the transition from individual to group-level prospective sensemaking". *Academy of Management Journal* 55: 1232–1259.

Strati, A. 1999. *Organization and Aesthetics*. London: Sage.

Strati, A. 2015. Aesthetics and Design: An Epistemology of the Unseen. In *The Routledge Companion to Philosophy in Organization Studies*, ed. R. Mir, H. Willmott, and M. Greenwood, 251–259. London: Routledge.

Taylor, S.S. 2018. Aesthetics, Emotions, and Logics. *Organizational Aesthetics* 8 (1): 1–4.

Wagemans, J. 2018. Perceptual Organization. In *The Stevens' Handbook of Experimental Psychology and Cognitive Neuroscience*: *Vol. 2. Sensation, Perception & Attention*, vol. ed. J. Serences and series ed. J.T. Wixted, Chapter 18, 803–872. Hoboken, NJ: Wiley.

Wasserman, V., and M. Frenkel. 2011. Organizational Aesthetics: Caught Between Identity Regulation and Culture Jamming. *Organization Science* 22 (2): 287–539.

Weick, K.E. 1995. *Sensemaking in Organizations*. Beverly Hills, CA: Sage.

Weick, K.E. 2001. *Making Sense of the Organization*. Malden, MA: Blackwell.

Yoo, Y., R. Boland, and K. Lytinen. 2006. From Organization Design to Organization Designing. *Organization Science* 17: 215–229.

PART III

Holistic Organization Designing (HOD)

The last part of the book covers the topic of organization designing and aims to explain how the holistic organization design model works in practice. It develops the three topics that make up the normative component—morality, collaboration and purpose—from the point of view of the *organization designer*, a managerial role which has hitherto not been part of the traditional roles of the manager. This managerial role was outlined earlier in the book, along with the suggestion that as an activity organization design should be split into two levels: a decentralized technical level and a holistic level. At the technical level, the aim is to ensure the efficiency and effectiveness of local artefact creation, in line with the principles and values behind the organization's purpose. Thus, purpose becomes the reference point for organization designing and as such there is a need to convert the intentions and expectations behind the statements of purpose into something tangible that organization designers can work with. Accomplishing the organization's purpose takes a unified effort involving the entirety of the organization, and this is where the holistic level is crucial. While at the operational level, the effort is detailed and analytical, at the holistic level, the approach becomes more like systemic sensing, requiring capabilities that are not only instrumental, but also aesthetic, that is, aestho-instrumental.

In order to provide a reasonable overview of the holistic level and of the capabilities required by HOD, let us go back to Barnard (1938) for a moment. In explaining the many sides of the "creative economy of the whole", he states:

> The creative side of organization is coordination (...) It goes by various roughly approximate names – 'all around management', 'executive perspective', 'practical sense of the whole', etc. (p. 256)

> The means utilized are to a considerable extent concrete acts logically determined, but the essential aspect of the process is the sensing of the organization as a whole. (p. 235)

> This general executive process is not intellectual, in its important aspect; it is aesthetic and moral. Its exercise involves the sense of fitness, of the appropriate and that capacity which is known as responsibility – the final expression for the achievement of cooperation". (p. 257)

The distinguishing mark of executive responsibility is that it requires not merely conformance to a complex code of morals but also the creation of moral codes for others [i.e.,] the process of inculcating points of view, fundamental attitudes, loyalties. (p. 279)

In these lines, Barnard provides an outline of the leadership qualities that are required from the holistic organization designer. First, he equates the creative side of organization to the phenomenon of coordination, and highlights that this approach to organization requires a holistic mindset, in tandem with "concrete acts" that are "logically determined". Second, he elects responsibility as a leadership requirement for upholding a sense of morality and cooperation throughout the organization. Third, in mentioning the necessity for executives to inspire fundamental attitudes and behaviours and creating "moral codes for for others", Barnard acknowledges a need for self-reflection among executives.

Hence, in this part of the book, we bring together the gist of the normative MCP framework discussed in Chapter 5 with the notion of holistic organization design, supported by Barnard's contribution, to propose three ideas that serve as the pillars of the new HOD role. Firstly, the idea that organizational coordination (and collaboration) is the aestho-instrumental outcome of the sharing of meanings and the creation of common understandings, where ethical and aesthetic capabilities are treated as complementary to the traditional rational-analytic competencies. Secondly, the notion that organizational purpose needs to be materialized in the form of a managerial tool that can generate commitment and a common language across all levels of management; the tool being suggested is the ethic-aesthetic vision. Thirdly, the converging qualities of aesthetic leadership, reflective practice and responsible management are suggested as the routes towards the successful achievement of the morality corner of MCP. This part of the book ends with a reflection about the need for reform of management education, if this vision of organization designing is to have any chance of success.

Reference

Barnard, C.I. 1938. *The Functions of the Executive*. Cambridge, MA: Harvard University Press.

CHAPTER 9

Aestho-Instrumental Coordination and the Ethic-Aesthetic Vision

Abstract Starting from a perspective of organization coordination as an essentially emergent phenomenon, anchored on common understandings and shared meanings, in this chapter it is argued that there is much in common between this perspective and our own conception of organization design-as-meaning. Also, attending to the cognitive and embodied characteristics of sensemaking, it can be assumed that common understandings and shared meanings also benefit from sensory or aesthetic knowledge, and that these provide a broader aestho-instrumental perspective to the phenomenon of coordination in organizations. This perspective is supported by authors who highlight that the *rational analytical* (i.e., instrumental) mode and the *aesthetic* mode are inseparable, insofar as they are both at work when people interact with the world. In other words, instrumental and aesthetic rationality are only distinguishable analytically, because in practice they occur simultaneously when members interact inside the organization or with the environment outside. The second part of the chapter discusses the notion of *ethic-aesthetic vision* as a way of materializing and presenting the organization's purpose, the assumption being that the choices of management about what to include and how to present and implement the organization's purpose not only reinforce or inhibit the organization's disposition towards morality and collaboration, but also determine the probability of the organization successfully reaching its social/environmental targets.

R. Magalhães, *Designing Organizations for the Betterment of Society*,
https://doi.org/10.1007/978-3-031-64483-2_9

Keywords Aesthetic mode · Aestho-instrumental · Coordination · Ethic-aesthetic · Instrumental mode · Purpose vision

Holistic Organization Design and the Aestho-Instrumental Nature of Organizational Coordination

Coordination is a core theme in organization theory, going all the way back to the origins of the discipline, with the early efforts to rationalize organizations from authors like by Frederick Taylor and Henry Fayol. The belief was that for organizations to function in rational ways, coordination was needed and that this could only be achieved through (instrumental) design, both the bottom-up design of work tasks and the top-down design of management systems. Through precise rules governing behaviour and well-designed roles prescribed independently of personal attributes or relations between individuals, it was assumed that such systems could be designed with such specificity and precision that individuals would complete their tasks in a quasi-automated manner. The outcome of decades of organization theory, however, has revealed that formalized, planned or engineered solutions often fail to provide acceptable coordination.

Weick (1969) is among the earliest management thinkers who have pointed out the fallacy of engineered recipes for organizational coordination, arguing instead that sensemaking is the best path for understanding coordinated organizing. In a major review of the literature, Okhuysen and Bechky (2009) contend that perspectives on organizational coordination have changed dramatically in the post-industrial age and that there is now a recognition that coordination is an *emergent phenomenon*. They explain coordination as a process of interaction, featuring three integrating conditions: accountability, predictability and common understanding. Lack of space precludes us from looking into each of these conditions, but *common understanding* is particularly relevant due to its close connections with sensemaking. They state:

> Common understanding helps coordinate by providing a shared perspective on the *whole task* and how individuals' work fits within the whole (ibid.:

488, italics added). Common understanding coordinates through interdependent parties developing a shared conception of the activities they are performing. Plans, rules, routines and familiarity create common understanding at the level of the whole interdependent task or work process. (ibid.: 489)

The emphasis on *holistic properties* indicates that coordination is an organizational phenomenon that requires more than the sharing of meaning about rational and instrumental elements of the task (i.e., the knowledge, the goals and the objectives of the work to be done, and how it is to be done), but also demands an element with aesthetic-holistic qualities. In a recent review of literature on organizational aesthetics, Baldessarelli et al. (2022) agree that there is value in integrating organizational aesthetics into the research on coordination. They explain that aesthetics plays an important role in the coordination process because of the elicited sensory reactions, as well as emotional and cognitive interpretations. In other words, aesthetics helps to understand how individuals collaborate and how the collective behaviour of people engaged in interdependent work is motivated by the emotional and rational perceptions, which are generated by the interactions with or through material artefacts. A number of authors reinforce this idea and contribute towards highlighting the role of aesthetics in organizational coordination.

Gagliardi (2006) discusses the coordination properties of the "pathos", an aesthetic quality characterized as a "pattern of sensibility", or the way organizational members perceive and feel reality. Pathos is part of a triad of rhetoric: the "logos" which pertains to cognitive experience, the "ethos" which concerns the experience of values and morals and the pathos as the element which conveys the aesthetic experience of a certain strategy of rhetoric. In rhetoric, the three elements work in tandem, alternating systematically and "with the regularity of breathing" (ibid.: 718) to provide the perfect articulation between intuition and rationalization, or between tacit and explicit. In a similar articulation, with the logos and the ethos, Gagliardi suggests that the pathos, as an aesthetic code of culture, is "an extraordinary resource for coordination" (ibid.: 713).

Creed et al. (2020) also claim that the aesthetic code has a role in organizational coordination. Under the notion of institutional aesthetics, these authors explain the aesthetic code as a system of shared values and sensibilities that governs the way people participate in institutional processes. And in a recent empirical study, Stephens (2021) provides an example of the role of aesthetic norms or codes in the achievement of organizational coordination. The study investigates the collective performance of an institutional group—a community choir—and features heed and collective mind as central concepts. It highlights not only how members of the choir persisted with the delivery of beautiful performances, but also how they continuously adapted their *coordinating behaviour* when they felt that collective performance was dwindling. In this study, Stephens also suggests that coordination is indeed an aestho-instrumental capability, in asserting that that embodied forms of cognition (i.e., what we know from direct experience of what is around us) complement representational forms of knowledge (i.e., what we know from symbols, or concepts).

The assumption that the sharing of meaning that lies behind the coordination phenomenon contains not only instrumental elements, but also aesthetic ones is further validated by the empirical work of Stigliani and Ravasi (2018) about the relevance of aesthetic knowledge for the work of designers. These authors conclude that aesthetic knowledge in organizations has a dual component—an element of aesthetic fluency and literacy and a component of declarative and procedural knowledge. Their work emphasizes the point that coordination in organizations does carry an aesthetic component, and that it is possible to share aesthetic knowledge integrating different types of knowledge inputs. From Stephens' case about the community choir, we see a similar conclusion in that to coordinate their action (i.e., the choir) group members had to integrate the stable and abstracted knowledge associated with material artefacts (i.e., the orchestra, the score), with the fluid and perceptual knowledge gained by direct experience of the choir's performance.

Aestho-Instrumental Coordination and Organization Design-as-meaning

Creed et al. (2020) highlight the distinction between the *rational analytical mode* (linear/sequential, intended, rational, calculative, reason-based) and the *aesthetic mode* (holistic/parallel, explorational, sensory, interpretive, emotional, embodied, visceral), the purpose of the former being to use the world for people's own benefits and uses, while the aim of latter is "to experience and relate to that world in the interest of *meaning making*" (ibid.: 419, italics added). They contend that while there is benefit in separating these two modes when analysing organizational events, they are indeed inseparable insofar as they are both at work when people interact with the world.

Shrivastava et al. (2017) make a similar distinction between the notions of instrumental and aesthetic rationality. They explain that aesthetic rationality should be understood as a type of value-oriented reasoning that supplements traditional instrumental reasoning in organizations. Instrumental rationality is characterized by the expectation that organizational members will always behave with the goal of maximizing overall utility (i.e., the choice of the most cost-effective alternative). The authors refer to aesthetic rationality as an "aesthetic-driven ethic" (ibid.: 369) that can potentially foster sustainability-sensitive behaviour in organizations and explain that the notions of instrumental and aesthetic rationality are only distinguishable analytically, because in practice they occur simultaneously when members interact inside the organization or with the outside world.

Thus, the notion of the aesthetic-instrumental nature of organizational coordination can be applied to the arguments presented in Part II about the new approach to organization design(ing) and about the holistic level as being essentially perceptual, sensory and cultural. Firstly, organizational coordination as an aesthetic-instrumental phenomenon feeds directly into our own conception of organization design-as-meaning, given that common understandings and shared meanings are defining features of both Weick's (1995) notion of sensemaking, and of Okhuysen and Bechky's (2009) description of coordination. Also, attending to the embodied and non-cognitive characteristics of sensemaking, it can be assumed that common understandings and shared meanings also benefit from sensory or aesthetic knowledge, and that these provide a significant contribution for a fuller understanding of the coordination phenomenon.

Additionally, in the light of the current trends on coordination and of the arguments put forward in Chapter 6, we recall the close interlinkage between the concepts of cooperation, collaboration and coordination, also highlighted in Bernacchio et al.'s (2022) definition of collaboration as "purposive coordination and cooperation, integrating heterogeneous inputs synergistically to create value" (ibid.: n/a). Consequently, it can be assumed that the three concepts move in unison, with coordination featuring as cause and effect of collaboration and cooperation. This is relevant because it not only highlights the way in which the triad MCP (morality-collaboration-purpose) contributes jointly to the normative system discussed earlier, but it also emphasizes the aestho-instrumental nature of the model as a whole.

Aestho-Instrumental Coordination at Core of the "Invisible Hand" of Dynamic Capabilities

In light of the above discussion about the aesthetic-instrumental nature of organizational coordination, we should now revisit Collis' (1994) proposal about the need to factor in organization culture and the relations among employees when trying to understand organizational capabilities, a phenomenon that Dosi et al. (2008) have compared to the invisible hand of the market. Firstly, it should be acknowledged that not every aspect of capabilities can be empirically tested, and that intuition and common sense based on experience also provide acceptable evidence for organizational behaviour. Indeed, authors such as Kay et al. (2018) suggest that dynamic capabilities are emergent and that they *co-evolve* with the organization's design. Moreover, they submit that the "orchestration" metaphor is a useful description of the emergent processes taking place between the different dynamic components of capabilities, but caution that orchestration "needs a conductor creatively coordinating the resulting assembly for a symphony to emerge, rather than a cacophony" (ibid.: 633).

Secondly, MacLean (2017) put forward that dynamic capabilities require aesthetic faculties, while Nayak et al. (2020) argue that the characteristics of capabilities which give organizations competitive potential (e.g., idiosyncrasy, tacitness or inimitability), cannot be fully explained by abstract information processing and conscious deliberation on the part of participants. Nayak et al. (2020) suggest that there is a need for a complementary framework for a thorough understanding of dynamic capabilities, featuring three non-cognitive properties: environmental affordances, empirical sensitivity and shared habitus. Environmental affordances refer to the background of possibilities that a participant has at her/his disposal while going about daily organizational life. They are fundamentally unspecifiable a priori, in the sense that their features may or may not be selected to produce novel components. Empirical sensitivity describes the capacity of a community for making refined discriminations of challenges presented by the environment and to determine what is best course of action; it is a capacity that is intuitive, and which cannot be captured linguistically. Habitus does not pre-suppose conscious cognition but refers to the active presence of past experiences in the form of "schemes of perception, thought and action, [that] guarantee the 'correctness' of practices and their constancy over time, more reliably than all formal rules and explicit norms" (Bourdieu 1990: 54).

Third, the non-cognitive or non-representational qualities put forward by Nayak et al. to explain the situated nature of dynamic capabilities matches our own model of organization design-as-meaning, while the cultural properties of the design gestalt provide further explanation for the coordination competencies encapsulated in the notion of dynamic capabilities. Through its embodied and aesthetic components, the design gestalt culture leads to the emergence of working contexts where technical and instrumental capabilities are allowed to intermesh with the habits, affordances and empirical sensitivities in ways that enable not only the job to be done, but also innovation to emerge. Such optimal conditions for the choreography and orchestration of organizational capabilities can also be labelled *organizational coordination*.

Summing up Coordination as an Output of Organization Designing

From the discussion so far, three important conclusions can be drawn. First, increasingly the topic of organizational coordination tends to be understood as a behavioural issue dependent on cooperation, collaboration, communication, meaning and aesthetic sensitivity. Secondly, based on this perspective on organization coordination, it is argued that there is much common with our own conception of organization design-as-meaning and that coordination can be seen as a natural output of organization designing. Also, attending to the cognitive and embodied characteristics of sensemaking, it can be assumed that common understandings and shared meanings also benefit from an aestho-instrumental perspective of the coordination phenomenon. Third, as a major example of an output of organization designing, we have put forward the case of dynamic capabilities and suggested that holistic organization design is the locus where the "magic" is achieved. In other words, it is suggested that the aestho-instrumental thinking of holistic organization design contains the missing answers for the invisible hand behind the choreography of organizational capabilities.

Ethic-Aesthetic Vision as the Materialization of Organizational Purpose

The MCP (morality-collaboration-purpose) triad is offered as the normative foundation of the overall design of organizations, irrespective of type, size, industrial sector or market demands. Morality and collaboration are generic characteristics that apply to every type of organization, but purpose is obviously different and needs to be adapted to each organization's choices, intent and strategy. Also, as we saw earlier in the text, there is an acknowledgement of the gaps that exist between the principles of morality espoused in the statements of the organization's purpose and the way intentions and promises are executed. Such gaps are part of the reasons why a new conceptualization of organization design is needed, and under the banner of holistic organization design, it is the job of the organization designer to work towards a narrowing of such gaps and ensure that both the purpose and the morality desiderata are achieved or upheld.

Also, the new understanding of organizational morality as virtue ethics has important implications in terms of our conception of organizational purpose. Adopting a normative stance, Dobson (2022) suggests that organizational purpose should be "directed toward nurturing reflective practices of aesthetic quality" (ibid.: 503). Notwithstanding its limited scope, in the sense that it refers only to the aesthetic quality of reflective practices, Dobson's statement must be placed in the broader context of organizational ethics and of the close connection between ethic and aesthetic judgments. As pointed out by Kerschbaum (2022), the knowledge that is embedded in the views of organizational stakeholders about their organization's performance is not only rational or analytic, but is also "felt" or "experienced", meaning that each stakeholder makes not only an aesthetic judgment, but also a moral one about how their organization is contributing to society (including their own quality of life). Such individual judgements and the organization's statement of purpose create a dialectic, which is reflected in the members' views about the organization's morality and therefore in their willingness to collaborate (see Fig. 6.2).

Given the systemic relationship between the elements of the MCP triad, it can be assumed that organizational purpose can be a cause and a consequence in holistic organization designing; Indeed, purpose can be a *catalyst,* however, its role will always depend on the choices that management will make about what to include and how to present and implement the organization's purpose. Thus, we posit that one way of presenting the organization's purpose is *through an ethic-aesthetic vision*. Based on a study of twelve design-oriented companies in Sweden, Venkatesh et al. (2012) put forward an innovative perspective on marketing strategy featuring an *aesthetic vision* anchored on design thinking. They suggest that such a strategy can only be achieved in the context of a top-down design orientation, where design becomes "the sum of all the company's activities", eventually embracing "all the finer details of the organization, its culture, people and practices" (ibid.: 302). In other words, an aesthetic vision implies a top management choice whereby design becomes "the driving force of the organization" (p. 289). Despite the marketing bias, such an articulation and its keen design orientation provides inspiration for more ambitious organization-wide statements of purpose, including the entirety of the organization's ESG (environmental, social and governance) aims and targets.

The work by Shrivastava et al. (2017) examining the likely implications of an aesthetic-driven ethic for sustainable behaviour and for performance in organizations, also provides important ideas about how ethical and aesthetic values can be integrated into the articulation of the organization's purpose. From this work, we have extracted and adapted Table 9.1. The table refers to an organization's sustainability-related objectives and includes a number of target areas distilled from the organization's ethic-aesthetic vision. It also shows that an aesthetic orientation does encompass ethical concerns, and that such an articulation of purpose can influence every aspect and every level of organizational life (i.e., strategy, systems, outputs and operations).

Thus, we suggest that the enactment of the new perspective on organization design can be aided by the articulation or the spelling out of organizational purpose as a statement like the aesthetic vision. Seen through the light of the organization design gestalt as a cultural construction, an aesthetic vision can have a strong impact not only in the culture but also in the experience of the organization. An aesthetic vision appeals to the sensible knowledge of organizational stakeholders (Kerschbaum 2022) and makes them more aware of the ethic-aesthetic implications of every aspect of organizational life. On the other hand, the literature on *leadership ethics suggests that* ethical behaviours are introduced by means of supportive contexts generated by *integrity based* programmes. Integrity-based programmes, as opposed to approaches based on compliance, aim to build moral character and guide sound moral judgements through values that are internalized by individual employees (Constantinescu and Kaptein 2020). Hence, an aesthetic vision can become a powerful tool for changing the ethos of the organization, making it more sensitive to issues of the environmental, social justice or quality of life.

Table 9.1 An example of the integration of ethical and aesthetic values under the umbrella of organizational purpose (with a focus on sustainability)

Elements of organizational purpose	*The aesthetic aspects*	*The ethical or moral aspects*	*Design and performance implications*
Overall vision	Harmony with stakeholders, nature and community. Balance among the "3Ps" (triple bottom line)	Ecologizing responsibility, concern for stakeholders	Better image, less conflict, more cooperation, collaboration
Strategy	Choice of clean businesses and technologies	Respect for nature, long-term survival, ecologizing constancy	Better image, improving long-term sustainability
Systems	Designing systems for beauty, in addition to efficiency. Humanizing the scale and size of systems	Economizing, concern for stakeholders	Smaller, less risky systems, facilitating internal cooperation, collaboration and coordination
Outputs (products and waste)	Beautiful products, compassionate services, recycling	Respect for nature, economizing, ecologizing constancy	Enhancing product competitiveness, lowering costs, improving community relationships
Operations	Attractive workspaces, grandeur in landscape and architecture	Respect for people and nature	Better image, making facilities more acceptable to communities

Source Adapted from Shrivastava et al. (2017)

References

Baldessarelli, G., I. Stigliani, and K.D. Elsbach. 2022. The Aesthetic Dimension of Organizing: A Review and Research Agenda. *Academy of Management Annals* 16: 217–257.

Barnard, C.I. 1938. *The Functions of the Executive*. Cambridge, MA: Harvard University Press.

Bernacchio, C., N.J. Foss, and S. Lindenberg. 2022. The Virtues of Joint Production: Ethical Foundations for Collaborative Organization. *Academy of Management Review*, published online: 8 September 2022.

Bourdieu, P. 1990. The Logic of Practice. Cambridge: Polity Press.

Collis, D.J. 1994. How Valuable Are Organizational Capabilities? *Strategic Management Journal* 15: 143–152.

Constantinescu, M., and M. Kaptein. 2020. Ethics Management and Ethical Management: Mapping Criteria and Interventions to Support Responsible Management Practice. In *The Research Handbook of Responsible Management*, ed. O. Laasch, R. Suddaby, R.E. Freeman, and D. Jamali. Cheltenham: E. Elgar.

Creed, W.E.D., S.S. Taylor, and B.A. Hudson. 2020. Institutional Aesthetics: Embodied Ways of Encountering, Evaluating, and Enacting Institutions. *Organization Studies* 41 (3): 415–435.

Dobson, J. 2022. Virtue Ethics, Aesthetics, and Reflective Practices in Business. *Philosophy of Management* 21: 493–505.

Dosi, G., M. Faillo, and L. Marengo. 2008. Organizational Capabilities, Patterns of Knowledge Accumulation and Governance Structures in Business Firms: An Introduction. *Organization Studies* 29: 1165–1185.

Gagliardi, P. 2006. Exploring the Aesthetic Side of Organizational Life. In *The Sage Handbook of Organizations Studies*, ed. S.R. Clegg, C. Hardy, T.B. Lawrence, and W.R. Nord. London: Sage.

Kay, N.M., S. Leih, and D.J. Teece. 2018. The Role of Emergence in Dynamic Capabilities: A Restatement of the Framework and Some Possibilities for Future Research. *Industrial and Corporate Change* 27 (4): 623–638.

Kerschbaum, C. 2022. A Beautiful Strategy: Bridging the Gap Between the (Aesthetic) Perception and (Strategic) Realization of the Organization's Purpose. *VINE Journal of Information and Knowledge Management Systems*, earlycite article, published 14 September 2022.

MacLean, D. 2017. Dynamic Capabilities, Creative Action, and Poetics. *Revista de Administração de Empresas-RAE* 57 (3): 264–272.

Nayak, A., Chia, R, & Canales, J. 2020. Noncognitive microfoundations: understanding dynamic capabilities as idiosyncractically refined sensitivities and predispositions. *Academy of Management Review* 45 (2): pp. 280–303.

Okhuysen, G.A., and B.A. Bechky. 2009. Coordination in Organizations: An Integrative Perspective. *The Academy of Management Annals* 3 (1): 463–502.

Shrivastava, P., G. Schumacher, D.M. Wasieleski, and M. Tasic. 2017. Aesthetic Rationality in Organizations: Toward Developing a Sensitivity for Sustainability. *The Journal of Applied Behavioural Science* 53 (3): 369–411.

Stephens, J.P. 2021. How the Show Goes On: Using the Aesthetic Experience of Collective Performance to Adapt While Coordinating. *Administrative Science Quarterly* 66 (1): 1–41.

Stigliani, I., and D. Ravasi. 2018. The Shaping of Form: Exploring Designers' Use of Aesthetic Knowledge. *Organization Studies* 39 (5–6): 747–784.

Venkatesh, A., T. Digerfeldt-Mansson, F.F. Brunel, and S. Chen. 2012. Design Orientation: A Grounded Theory Analysis of Design Thinking and Action. *Marketing Theory* 12 (3): 289–309.

Weick, K.E. 1969. *The Social Psychology of Organizing*. Reading, MA: Addison-Wesley.
Weick, K.E. 1995. *Sensemaking in Organizations*. Beverly Hills, CA: Sage.

CHAPTER 10

Organizational Morality Through Aesthetic Leadership, Reflective Practice and Responsible Management

Abstract In the previous chapter, two of the prongs of the MCP triad—collaboration/coordination and purpose—were developed. In the present chapter, the third prong—morality—is the focus of attention, in the context of the role of *organization designer*, a managerial role which has hitherto not been part of the traditional roles of management. In this chapter, a link between organization design-as-meaning and the processes of leading-through-meanings or aesthetic leadership, as well as reflective practice and responsible management are established, as the paths towards organizational morality and a new ethic-aesthetic mindset. However, for this to happen, something must be done to the way managers are educated and trained. Thus, the chapter ends with a call for much-needed reform in traditional management education, and a change in the mindset of management educators, if the new ambitions about organizational purpose are to have any chance of flourishing. The key message here is that as MOS academics, we need to *transform ourselves before we can transform societies*. For a few decades, there has been a claim from the literature about a need for thorough reform of management education, but now more than ever, practising managers need to have a different perspective of their role in society, and moral excellence, coupled with a new ethic-aesthetic perspective on organization design(ing) can provide an important impetus towards that end.

R. Magalhães, *Designing Organizations for the Betterment of Society*,
https://doi.org/10.1007/978-3-031-64483-2_10

Keywords Aesthetic leadership · Character · Ethic-aesthetic · Leadership · Moral excellence · Reflective practice · Responsible management · Virtuous

In the previous chapter, we have developed two of the prongs of the MCP triad—collaboration/coordination and purpose—the normative foundation of organization design in the present chapter, we conclude our proposal about the paradigm of ***holistic organization designing***, with some additional considerations about third prong—morality. New pressures on organizations bring fresh directions in managerial practice, in the form of a new balance between the societal dimension of their responsibilities and the traditional concerns with organizational effectiveness and market competitiveness. New ESG (environmental, social and governance) concerns have begun to emerge in the literature, in response to the global warming, social inequalities and the COVID crisis, with calls from academia for corporations to rethink and reform the way they perceive, articulate and implement their purpose (George et al. 2023; Nonaka and Takeuchi 2021). Such calls emphasize higher order purposes that link the business to its moral and ethical obligations. The following citation provides a good synthesis of the commonalities between such new directions in management thought and our own proposals for a change in the organization design paradigm:

> Economic prosperity in the future solely depends on a social ecosystem of knowledge. The practice of co-creation will lead to the realization of a society of the "Good Life," as Aristotle put it (...) Knowledge is created out of relationships. Through intersubjectivity, stakeholders involved in knowledge creation dynamically create and change their relationships. In successive years, a firm must involve society as a whole in this knowledge creation process, dissolve organizational boundaries, and cooperate and co-create with others in an open manner. Through active engagement with the world, a firm can promote the development of a *moral society*. (Nonaka and Yamaguchi 2022: 213, italics added)

In this citation, where a philosophical stance akin to MacIntyre's virtue ethics can be detected, the call is for organizations to assume a different level of responsibility in their societal role and aim towards a higher good in the search for economic prosperity. On the other hand, the citation suggests that there is a connection between responsibility, morality and knowledge creation through the development of intersubjectivity (meanings). This is in line with our hypothesis of organization design-as-meaning, where it is suggested that organization design can be defined as the creation and development of the meanings of interactions, relationships and experiences mediated by organizational artefacts, culminating with the organization as the artefact-of-artefacts. Considering that many of the meanings have ethic-aesthetic connotations, it can be assumed that *morality in organizations is closely tied to the development of the organization's design.*

In this chapter, we will establish the link between organization design-as-meaning and the processes of leading-through-meanings or aesthetic leadership, as well as reflective practice and responsible management, as the paths towards organizational morality and a new ethic-aesthetic mindset. However, for this to happen, something must be done to the way managers are educated and trained. Thus, the chapter ends with a call for much-needed reform in traditional management education, and a change in the mindset of management educators, if the new ambitions about the role of organizational purpose are to have any chance of flourishing.

Aesthetic (and Moral) Leadership

According to Nonaka and Yamaguchi's (2022) theory of the firm, the development of meanings in the organization is regarded as an important component of knowledge creation, the resource which enables organizations to grow, prosper and become competitive. Given that the development of meanings takes place mainly at the level of intersubjective sensemaking, leaders should foster the *development of intersubjectivity* by means of nurturing the organizational conditions through which people can interface and build relationships that reciprocally influence each other.

This process starts from the moment that someone joins an organization, and meanings begin to be formed from day one. In fulfilling their roles in the organization and in guiding their subordinates, managers are constantly creating meaning in a variety of ways, for example, by suggesting new way of executing the task, by providing examples of how to solve problems or by spelling out procedures that had previously remained implicit. Smircich and Morgan (1982: 262) propose that such management of meaning lies at the core of the art of leadership and that as organizations mature, patterns of desired meanings become institutionalized, and specific frames or "contexts of meaning" begin to emerge. The process of creating contexts of meaning has also been labelled as *authoring* (Shotter 1993). Shotter puts forward that one of the manager's tasks is to author conversations by converting abstract problem situations into clear discourse, making sense of seemingly disorderly events, creating coherent explanatory structures and conveying her interpretations to organizational audiences. This idea was picked up by Weick (1995: 8) in explaining that the concept of sensemaking "is about authoring, as well as interpretation, creation and discovery" (Ibid, p. 8).

Thus, the manager-leader at work is a sense-giver, providing others with a sense of meaning about the tasks at hand, but he is also a sense-adapter in so far as he needs to interpret and discover the meanings emerging from improvised design throughout the organization. Indeed, the process of leading-through-sense-and-meaninghas been highlighted by authors other than Smircich and Morgan (1982). For example, Pye (2005: 31) suggests that leadership should be understood as a sense-making process, while Cunliffe and Eriksen (2011: 1432) argue that leadership is a relational and "broadly hermeneutic" process, "embedded in everyday experience". Importantly, Cunliffe and Eriksen also highlight that leadership is "interwoven with a sense of moral responsibility" (Ibid, p. 1432).

Leading-through-sense-and-meanings relies mostly on the use of language; however, there is another level of meanings which also contribute to the development of the organization's system of meanings, i.e., "felt" meanings (Warren 2008). That being the case, it might be proposed that leadership also has an important aesthetic dimension. Indeed, arguing from the point of view that leadership cannot be reduced to the measurement of psychological factors, Hansen et al. (2007) point out that people do not use only rationality and intellect in making personal and work-related decisions, but also utilize their bodies, as well as emotions, feelings and personal experiences, which cannot be represented in any rational models. Indeed, these authors emphasize that "it is in those situations where rationality does not apply that leadership is most crucial. If we could reduce every decision to a rational model, we would not need leaders at all" (ibid.: 549). Leadership aesthetics focuses on how leadership phenomena emerge and attempts to describe *felt meanings* as they are experienced by both leaders and followers. It is an approach that "enables us to study and to talk about the subtle, underlying qualities, which we sense, but cannot quite put our finger on" (Hansen et al. 2007: 552). Felt meanings flow from aesthetic perceptions as the raw, unfiltered sense our bodies are constantly picking up. Hence, in order to decide what is important to attend to, aesthetic leaders need to develop their aesthetic sensibility.

Aesthetic sensibility is about the intuitive grasp of the non-rational, sensory and affective elements of daily situations. Ladkin (2018) suggests that aesthetic sensibility requires *integrative apprehension*, a perception category which is the outcome of three components: perceptual enhancement, emotional connection and imaginative capacity. Perceptual enhancement concerns the ability to perceive the organizational whole by considering how the various relevant aspects to a situation relate to one another, how tensions are resolved and how a balancing point might be reached. Emotional connection refers to the fact that both aesthetic sensibility and ethical deliberation depend on the ability to engage emotionally, highlighting the point that in order for our aesthetic and ethical sensibilities to be aroused and empathetic engagement to ensue, emotional engagement is a requirement. In other words, emotions trigger our aesthetic experiences. Imaginative capacity is closely related to emotional connection, but takes it a step further, in the sense that aesthetic sensitivity allows us to step into the other person's shoes and build (i.e., imagine) possible scenarios around the person's circumstances.

So, aesthetic sensibility is part of the skills that give the organization designer "professional judgment based on cultivated sensitivity' (Ewenstein and Whyte 2007: 701), a "must have" for navigating and sensing complex systems and forming a holistic perspective of organizational events. Moreover, Ladkin (2018) remarks that *aesthetic sensibility* and *ethical judgement* are key ingredients of holistic sensing capability, which leads us to conclude that an increased awareness of the morality of daily organizational issues is also a requirement of aesthetic leadership. Therefore, leaders equipped with the skills of perceptual enhancement, emotional connection and imaginative capacity will be better able to understand the issues of holistic organization design(ing) and contribute towards the moral ambitions of organizational purpose. A drive towards morality can also be enhanced if leaders are aware of the need for reflective practice and responsible management.

Reflective Practice and Responsible Management

Influenced by MacIntyre's (2007) virtue ethics, Cunliffe (2009) argues that leadership as a moral activity is ***not*** about having a code of ethics or about training people to act in ethical ways, but about *who you are in your role as a manager (or non-manager)*. Similarly, Hibbert and Cunliffe (2015) posit that responsible management entails moral agency and the realization that our lives are shaped with others, and that in shaping our lives we need to critically examine our relationships with others. These authors restate that aesthetic reflexive practice is not "some anodyne and cerebral activity" (ibid.: 184), but something that involves an aesthetic and embodied engagement. Aesthetic reflexive practice can be sparked, for example, by a question that should concern any manager, i.e., "what type of institution do I want to create and to be a part of?" Through questions like this, managers are continually reminded that the impact on the world of the organizations they design and manage is their responsibility. And responsibility requires character, a leadership quality explained by Cunliffe and Eriksen (2011) in the following way:

> Character is embedded and expressed within conversations not as traits or constructs, but as a way of being-in-relation-to-others that brings a moral responsibility to treat people as human beings, of having 'a heart', appreciating others, and encouraging them to grow and learn from each other. (ibid.: 1433)

Therefore, character can also be *institutional*. In fact, Sudabby describes institutional character as a kind of organizational commitment to a set of enduring and universal humanistic values and "ontological givens" that define humanity, such as love, justice, fairness, trust, compassion or dignity (in Carroll et al. 2020: 70). At this point, it must be noted that there is interesting complementarity between the characteristics of individual character at the micro-level and institutional character at the macro-level, and the processes of sensemaking that lead to the organization design gestalt, as the macro-level in our model. Sensemaking, to include cognitive and rational information processing, as well as non-cognitive, sensory and intuitive perception is indeed the substance of organization design, but reflexivity is what provides morality to the processes of sensemaking. Cunliffe (2016) helps to articulate this idea by stating that "embracing intersubjectivity, relationality, and reflexivity brings a *moral responsibility* to think about 'we' not 'I' in our relationships and responsibility for the world around us" (ibid.: 743, italics added).

Reflexivity and moral responsibility come together under Dobson's (2022) notion of reflective practice, which he defines as "an aesthetic space or clearing that enables practitioners to reflect, in a non-prejudicial way, on the true nature of the practice in which they are engaged" (ibid.: 495). By non-prejudicial, he means that "the virtues embraced by the practice are not premised upon, or pre-judged by the institution that houses the practice" (ibid.: 495). Thus, he clarifies that members engaged in the practice have an institutional responsibility towards their organization, but at the same time they have a personal responsibility to reflect upon and exercise the virtues, while fulfilling their institutional responsibility. Hence, the truly virtuous manager is one who assumes and accepts both type of types of responsibility, with responsible management emerging as a quality that is associated with managers' moral reflective practice. To recap, Dobson argues that in an organizational setting the defining characteristic of practices lies beyond excellence and is defined by a capacity for reflection in the pursuit of an *aesthetic ideal.*

To recap, Dobson argues that in an organizational setting the defining characteristic of practices lies beyond excellence and is defined by a capacity for reflection in the pursuit of an aesthetic ideal. Given the close intertwinement between ethical and aesthetic judgements made by the human mind, we suggest that the type of knowledge which activates the sensitivity required by management practitioners to make judgements about "the good" is the same as the knowledge behind judgements about "the beauty" of organizational experiences. According to Strati (2020), the combination of "the beauty" and "the good" as elements of organizational life is the basis of *responsible management*. On the other hand, Ladkin (2018) explains that both aesthetics and ethics are ways of knowing, and that critical reflexivity is a significant individual feature that mediates between aesthetic values and the ability of people to behave ethically.

Concluding

The following points summarize the key issues about the complementary and mutually reinforcing relationship between morality and organization design(ing), through aesthetic leadership, reflective practice and responsible management.

1. Organization designing requires the mastering of holistic management capabilities, which in turn, entails, not only an understanding of systems, but also the personal development of aesthetic sensitivity and aesthetic leadership skills.
2. Aesthetic leadership has a great deal in common with organization designing, in the sense that both focus on felt and rational meanings, and in both the management of meaning occupies a central position.
3. But aesthetic leadership also contains a moral element, which can only come to the surface by means of reflexivity and moral responsibility on part of the practitioners. Additionally, the notion of morality as reflective practice supports the Morality-Collaboration-Purpose triad, the normative component of our organization design model.
4. According to Dobson's interpretation of virtue ethics, organizational members have an institutional responsibility to help the organization in achieving its objectives, but at the same time they have a personal responsibility to live a life of virtue. This duality, at the level of the individual, means that achieving the organization's purpose depends on the actions of virtuous managers, but at the organizational level, it means that morality-inducing organizational designs are required for achieving the organization's purpose.

Transforming Ourselves to Transform Societies

Many of the ideas put forward in this book do not conform to the dominant paradigm in management theory or practice. However, there is also a growing awareness among practitioners that something (or many things) has to change if organizations are to play their part in the solution of the environmental, social and economic problems that most parents would not like to leave as their legacy to their children. Hence, to wrap up this chapter, we have chosen to highlight the need for reform of the hard-nosed and purely instrumental mindset of managers.

To this end, we have found inspiration in the title of a chapter by Merino and Díaz (2022) about the merits of virtue ethics as the means for higher education to play its part in a more just and sustainable world. The authors argue that the development of virtuous thinking, feeling and acting is key for an education system geared towards sustainability and the common good. They suggest that education systems, at least in the

Western world, might be accused of contributing to unsustainable living, because they contribute to the societal structures that allow and promote unsustainable lifestyles. Merino and Díaz posit that in general, higher education institutions do not provide the forum for reflection, discussion and action that would enable learners to become sufficiently aware of the challenges posited by sustainability and to propose virtue ethics as the way forward in the development of the moral and political consciousness that are required to bring about change in the prevailing educational paradigm.

Transforming ourselves to become more virtuous implies reflexivity, an essential condition to engage with change, whether it is change at the personal level or aimed at the social context (Hibbert 2013; Hibbert et al. 2019). A better future through reflective practice implies personal responsibility. Managers, as creators of the organization's present and future, have the moral obligation to consider the stakeholders, and the best way for managers to achieve the required sensitivity to understand the sentiments of care and empathy towards others and nature is through the mastering of virtues. In the literature, there is no agreement on the set of virtues that should be taught to management students, and related research has failed to produce a list of commonly accepted virtues, either managerial or organizational (Constantinescu and Kaptein 2020); however, as suggested by Sison and Ferrero (2015), rather than a specific set of values, what is important is that the organization develop skills of virtuousness and moral excellence in everything it does.

Thus, *transforming ourselves through virtues and moral character* is the recommendation that we would like to end up with, regarding a requirement that we see as the essential requirement for the implementation of the new model of organization design. This entails sensitizing managers (and especially future managers) about organization design as a topic that is simultaneously rational and non-rational in nature. Managers need to be taught that organization design is much wider than organizational structure and that it encompasses the organization as a whole, including its ethic-aesthetic foundations. To achieve this, there is need for a reform of minds in management and management education, and for managers and educators to adopt a fresh perspective on the analysis of organizational performance, allowing sensory or aesthetic inputs, alongside the traditional quantitative methods. But, most importantly, there is need for a new attitude of moral imagination, instead of one of utilitarian morality (Patriotta and Starkey 2008).

Utilitarian morality refers to an instrumental attitude to learning, where knowledge is valued, not for its intrinsic worth, but because of what it produces, i.e., individual value, better jobs, more status, etc. Such a view of knowledge provides efficiency, standardization and recipes for "more of the same", but it leads to superficial understanding. Moral imagination, on the other hand, starts from the premise that education should cultivate imagination and experimentation, as much as analysis, with a sharp focus on how one's actions will affect the fate of others. In other words, moral imagination opens the door to the transformation of the world, but it requires our own transformation through the development of virtues and moral character.

References

Carroll, A.B., N.J. Adler, H. Mintzberg, F. Cooren, R. Suddaby, R.E. Freeman, and O. Laasch. 2020. What 'Are' Responsible Management? A Conceptual Potluck. In *The Research Handbook of Responsible Management*, ed. O. Laasch, R. Suddaby, R.E. Freeman, and D. Jamali. Cheltenham: E. Elgar.

Constantinescu, M., and M. Kaptein. 2020. Ethics Management and Ethical Management: Mapping Criteria and Interventions to Support Responsible Management Practice. In *The Research Handbook of Responsible Management*, ed. O. Laasch, R. Suddaby, R.E. Freeman, and D. Jamali. Cheltenham: E. Elgar.

Cunliffe, A. L. 2009. The Philosopher Leader: "on relationalism, ethics and reflexivity-a critical perspective to teaching leadership. *Management Learning*, 40 (1): 87–101

Cunliffe, A.L. 2016. On Becoming a Critically Reflexive Practitioner Redux: What Does It Mean to *Be* Reflexive? *Journal of Management Education* 40 (6): 740–746.

Cunliffe, A.L., and M. Eriksen. 2011. Relational Leadership. *Human Relations* 64 (11): 1425–1449.

Dobson, J. 2022. Virtue Ethics, Aesthetics, and Reflective Practices in Business. *Philosophy of Management* 21: 493–505.

Ewenstein, B., and J. Whyte. 2007. Beyond Words: Aesthetic Knowledge and Knowing in Organizations. *Organization Studies* 28 (05): 689–708.

George, G., Haas, M. R., McGahan, A. M., Schillebeeckx, S. J. D., & Tracey, P. 2023. Purpose in the For-Profit Firm: a review and framework for management research. *Journal of Management*, 49 (6): 1841–1869

Hansen, H., A. Ropo, and E. Sauer. 2007. Aesthetic Leadership. *The Leadership Quarterly* 18: 544–560.

Hibbert, P. 2013. Approaching Reflexivity Through Reflection: Issues for Critical Management Education. *Journal of Management Education* 37 (6): 803–827.

Hibbert, P., and A. Cunliffe. 2015. Responsible Management: Engaging Moral Reflexive Practice Through Threshold Concepts. *Journal of Business Ethics* 127: 177–188.

Hibbert, P., L. Callagher, F. Siedlok, C. Windahl, and H.S. Kim. 2019. (Engaging or Avoiding) Change Through Reflexive Practices. *Journal of Management Inquiry* 28 (2): 187–203.

Ladkin, D. 2018. The Aesthetic and Its Relationship to Business Ethics: Philosophical Underpinnings and Implications for Future Research. *Journal of Business Ethics* 147: 35–51.

MacIntyre, A. 2007. *After Virtue*, 3rd ed. London: Duckworth.

Merino, A., and E. Díaz. 2022. Transforming Ourselves to Transform Societies: Cultivating Virtue in Higher Education for Sustainability. In *The Wiley Handbook of Sustainability in Higher Education Learning and Teaching*, ed. K.A. Gamage and N. Gunawardhana. New York: Wiley.

Nonaka, I., and H. Takeuchi. 2021. Humanizing Strategy. *Long Range Planning* 54 (4): 102070.

Nonaka, I., and I. Yamaguchi. 2022. *Management by Eidetic Intuition: A Dynamic Management Theory Predicated on the "Philosophy of Empathy."* London: Palgrave Macmillan.

Patriotta, G., and K. Starkey. 2008. From Utilitarian Morality to Moral Imagination: Reimagining the Business School. *Journal of Management Inquiry* 17 (4): 319–327.

Pye, A. 2005. Leadership and Organizing: Sensemaking in Action. *Leadership* 1 (1): 31–50.

Shotter, J. 1993. *Conversational Realities: Constructing Life Through Language*. London: Sage.

Sison, A.J.G., and I. Ferrero. 2015. How Different Is Neo-Aristotelian Virtue from Positive Organizational Virtuousness? *Business Ethics: A European Review* 24: 78–98.

Smircich, L., and G. Morgan. 1982. Leadership: The Management of Meaning. *Journal of Applied Behavioural Science* 18 (3): 257–273.

Strati, A. 2020. Beauty of Responsible Management: The Lens and Methodology of Organizational Aesthetics. In *The Research Handbook of Responsible Management*, ed. O. Laasch, R. Suddaby, R.E. Freeman, and D. Jamali. Cheltenham: E. Elgar.

Warren, S. 2008. Empirical Challenges in Organizational Aesthetics Research: Towards a Sensual Methodology. *Organization Studies* 29 (4): 559–580.

Weick, K.E. 1995. *Sensemaking in Organizations*. Beverly Hills, CA: Sage.

CHAPTER 11

Conclusion

Abstract This chapter contains an overview of the book, arranged in three blocks: the normative, the ontological and the dual-level organizational designing block. The normative bock is about the MCP (morality-collaboration-purpose) triad. Using it as a conceptual tool, organization design(ing) is about embedding the values and principles implicit or explicit in the organization's purpose into the organization's fabric. The MCP triad hinges around the notion of organizational morality and represents a chain of causes and effects working at individual level. The ontological block is about the hypothesis of organization design-as-meaning. It proposes that organization design, as perceived and experienced by internal and external stakeholders, is always the outcome of sensemaking, in a process that aggregates from the level of intersubjective meanings to the cultural level of the design gestalt. It defines organization design as an *evolving process of understanding, not only for organizational members as they organize around common tasks, routines or practices, but also for external stakeholders as they try to make sense of the organization and its peculiarities*. The last block considers organization design(ing) from a managerial viewpoint and suggests that it should be split into two sub-topics: (i) the design of local operational artefacts, which includes the design, implementation, updating and/or maintenance of artefacts from all functional areas; and (ii) the holistic design of the organization as a quasi-natural sociomaterial artefact.

R. Magalhães, *Designing Organizations for the Betterment of Society*,
https://doi.org/10.1007/978-3-031-64483-2_11

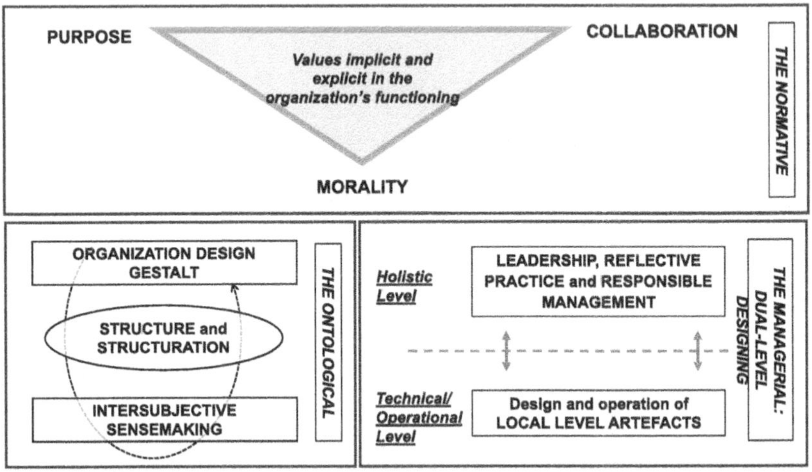

Fig. 11.1 Summarizing the new approach to organization design(ing) in three blocks

Keywords Culture · Dual-level · External stakeholders · Holistic design · MCP triad · Normative · Ontological

Figure 11.1 contains an overview of the book, arranged in three blocks: the normative, the ontological and the dual-level organizational designing block. Each block will be addressed in turn, with a final conclusion to be drawn under the heading of *the ethic-aesthetic scaffold*.

The Normative Block

We started this book by drawing attention to the need for a repositioning of the field of organization design, primarily due to the absence of an ethic-normative ambition in the paradigm that has ruled research and teaching in the field for the last half-century. This reflects a highly reductionistic interpretation of the concept of design by the contingency school of thought, coupled with the domination of the field by an economics bias. Such shortcomings have led to a feeling of dissatisfaction in parts of the academic world about the clear inability of organization design, as a topic of research and practice, to respond to new challenges of organization.

The repositioning starts from the assumption that organization design will always be dependent upon the strategic choices and decisions from the organization's owners, founders or high-level stewards in the case of public-sector organizations about their *purpose*. Global warming, social inequalities and the recent impact of the COVID-19 pandemic on the global economy have brought to the fore the need for a new attitude from profit and non-profit organizations about their *purpose*, and the role they should be playing in bringing about solutions. This means that as organizations move focus on purpose as a strategic concern aiming at the betterment of stakeholders, the environment and society in general (George et al. 2023), the more amenable the idea that design (and therefore morality, collaboration and purpose) should serve as a tool for steering organizations towards what they *could be*.

In proposing how to move forward and rescue a concept that can still be of great relevance to MOS, we have firstly turned to the design discipline for inspiration regarding the foundational principles of design and especially of human-centred design. The first principle to be observed derives from very definition of design as the study of artefacts (or the science of the artificial) and from the facts that organizations are made up of myriad artefacts. The other two principles that are also highly applicable to organization design are design-as-meaning and design-as-ethics. In fact, the three principles can be merged into one—human-centred design—as the new trend in design studies, a trend that has gained currency especially through the work of Krippendorff (2006). Accordingly, the content of a design cannot be obtained from the artefact itself but needs to be sought from the meanings constructed by the receiver in her contact with the design. Without an understanding of the receiver's inferred meaning, the content or the effects of the artefact cannot be known.

Once organization design is defined as the creation and change of meanings, and the concept of meaning is made to encompass non-cognitive sensemaking, morality falls into place as an organization design topic. In other words, the development of morality in the organization is tied to the development of its design, and vice-versa. Using the MCP (morality-collaboration-purpose) triad as the normative foundation, organization design(ing) is about embedding the values and principles implicit or explicit in the organization's purpose into the organization's fabric.

The triad hinges around the notion of organizational morality and represents a chain of causes and effects working at individual level. Morality is defined in terms of Dobson's (2022) version of MacIntyre's virtue ethics, a perspective that blends ethics and aesthetics. Accordingly, morality is something self-reflective, centred on a dual responsibility, i.e., an institutional responsibility for making work processes more efficient, and a personal responsibility to exercise the virtues in the pursuit of excellence.

As regards organizational purpose, this component of the triad should be understood as the personal outcome of a dialectic between the set of values contained *in the organization's stated purpose* and *the perception of each organizational member* about the execution of said purpose (which, in turn, is defined by the individual's personal virtuosity). Such a dialectic affects the individual's motivation at work, including the will to collaborate. The concepts of cooperation, collaboration and coordination are tightly interlinked and jointly contribute to the type of purpose that the organization is capable of achieving. Thus, the holistic level of organization design(ing) is proposed as a cultural gestalt, which stands behind the organization's capacity for achieving *both* its ethic-aesthetic ambitions and its competitive aims.

Although most organizations explicitly espouse purposes (especially on non-economic issues) which are laudable, for the large majority purpose statements are, in practice, no more than wishful lists of good intentions. The consequence of this is the permanent state of dissonance described above between individual morality and the political and economic machinations of corporate decision-making. This imbalance causes most organizations to be lopsided in very fundamental ways. The solution proposed in this book is to formalize organization design(ing) as a role charged with evening out the imbalance by *gradually embedding an ethic-aesthetic ethos* into the organization's sociomaterial fabric. The emphasis on morality-as-virtuosity-and-excellence and the drive towards the common good have the potential to create a powerful internal push for statements of organizational purpose to become ever more genuine.

The Ontological Block

The hypothesis of organization design-as-meaning is the ontological component of the model. It proposes organization design as the way that organizational features are *perceived* and *experienced* by internal and external stakeholders, which means that organization design is always the outcome of sensemaking, in processes that aggregates from the level of intersubjective meanings to the cultural level of the design gestalt. In other words, the hypothesis of organization design-as-meaning explains how organization design is

> an *evolving process of understanding*, not only for organizational members as they organize around common tasks, routines or practices, but also for external stakeholders as they try to make sense of the organization and its peculiarities.

The process starts at the intersubjective level, where members build their understanding of the organization's design by interacting with each other, with and through the available artefacts. As explained by several authors, the materiality of organizational artefacts becomes embedded and embodied in the sensemaking processes that unfold during the intersubjectivity of member interactions. Thus, it can safely be asserted that all intersubjectivity is mediated by organizational artefacts and that all subsequent stages of organization design-as-meaning are artefact-mediated. The next stage concerns organizational structure and structuration, where the key idea is that structure is not something static governed solely by formal rules and regulations; it is a social construction with emotional and temporal dimensions. The possibility of analysing and monitoring the type and quality of interactions gives organization design a new tool for managing structural arrangements in very innovative ways.

The last stage of organization design-as-meaning—the organization design gestalt—is conceptualized as a cultural construction that shapes myriad organizational *contexts*, which organizational members use to attribute meanings to artefacts, interactions and relationships. The organization design gestalt provides an instrument for the promotion of alignment between interactions, relationships and experiences in/of the organization and the morality subsumed by the organization's stated purpose. Types of organizational experiences for internal and external stakeholders are experiences of fairness, of justice, of compassion, of sympathy, of empathy or of approachability.

Hence, once organization designing is defined as the creation of meaning, designing, sensemaking and organizing are inevitably intertwined. The manager-leader is the first *sense-giver* at work, providing organizational members with a sense of meaning about the tasks at hand.

But organization design is also about the meanings of organizational artefacts, i.e., meanings for *those who take decisions and initiate action* in the pursuit of organizational objectives, as well as *for the people using or affected by the artefacts*. Thus, the meanings mediated or influenced by organizational artefacts affect *interactions*, *relationships* and *experiences* throughout the organization. The pervasive influence of organizational artefacts on organizational life remains a black box in organizational analysis, which the present book will, hopefully, begin to unveil.

The Dual-Level Organizational Designing Block

From a managerial viewpoint, organization design(ing) naturally splits into two sub-topics: (i) the design of local operational artefacts, with special attention to the role of the organization designer in providing interpretations and situated understandings about definitions, meanings and approaches in line with the principles and values behind the organization's purpose; and (ii) the holistic design of the organization as a quasi-natural (McKelvey 1997) sociomaterial artefact.

The level of operational artefacts includes the policies, systems or procedures from all functional areas of the organization, and concerns the design, implementation, updating and/or maintenance of artefacts carried out by internal and external providers in a decentralized and mostly uncoordinated fashion. In large organizations, many of these local-level artefacts are outsourced to consulting companies, sometimes only for purposes of design and implementation, and other times for operation as well. Although the principal (i.e., the commissioning organization) keeps a degree of control over the execution of the outsourcing contract, there are many unintended consequences of the implementation of the contracted artefacts, which remain outside the control of the principal, but still affect both internal and external stakeholders. All local level artefacts become part of overall organization design, sometimes with important implications for the quality of interactions and the relationships among stakeholders, as well as the organization's image. In brief, outsourcing has major implications for design, performance and experiences of the organization.

As Barnard (1958) had predicted more than 60 years ago, the moral factor involved in the adoption of new organizational artefacts (mostly digitally based, nowadays) continues to be substantially neglected. The *lack of regard for the design of local-level organizational artefacts* has important moral, social, environmental and economic consequences, all exerting different types of pressures, jointly combining to force the organization to veer away from its stated purpose. Artefacts have largely acquired a "will of their own", and it has become customary to hear in organizations that "the system" or "the legacy" are the reason why this or that cannot be done. However, it must also be highlighted that it is not feasible to try and manage local level artefacts from the top. The design of organizational artefacts has become highly specialized, with service providers emerging to serve each of the different functional areas of finance, operations, marketing, HR or top management offering very specific or even bespoke products or services. Thus, what organizations can (and should) do to tackle the problem is to extend the notion of general management to encompass holistic organization design as a new managerial incumbency.

Tackling the challenge of holistic thinking requires managerial competencies with innovative features. It requires an aesthetics mindset to enable managers to understand stakeholders' ethic-aesthetic experiences, as well as to respond to "the subtle, underlying qualities, which we sense, but cannot quite put our finger on" (Hansen et al. 2007: 552). Such sensing is holistic, in the sense that it cannot be pinned down to a specific cause or a particular consequence. This competency is part of *aesthetic leadership*, a skill set that might be described as leading-as-managing-meaning. It deals with different types of meaning, namely conventional meanings relying on language and discourse, as well as felt meanings. The first type is broadly covered by the topic of organizational communication, with a special focus on the exploitation, handling influencing, manoeuvring or shaping of meaning, at all stages of the designing process.

Aesthetic leadership deals also with felt meanings and therefore *aesthetic sensitivity* is a required capability for the organization designer. Among other components, aesthetic sensitivity is developed through self-reflexivity, an important component of morality and responsible leadership. Responsible management entails moral agency and the realization that our lives are shaped with others, and that in shaping our lives we need not only to have character, but also to be aware of our relationships with others. Lastly, *aesthetic vision* is also a tool that requires holistic thinking competencies. It is a strategic management tool that requires a good grasp of the ethic-aesthetic implications of organizational purpose as the driving force behind the organization's ESG (environmental, social and governance) aims and targets. The aesthetic vision implies a top-down design orientation, but above all it requires the organization to have a scaffold that can support such a vision.

The Ethic-Aesthetic Scaffold

Over time, different areas of management expertise, such as marketing, finance, operations or strategy have developed foundational scaffolds, which provide organizations with the ground rules. For example, in marketing the four Ps are foundational and strategy is anchored on frameworks like SWOT and Porter's five forces. However, in the areas of morality, governance or social responsibility, organizations operate *without a scaffold*, which becomes clear, for example, when management educators are engaged in the teaching of the societal role of organizations. Unfortunately, the ethics and aesthetics of management and organization are still largely a blackhole in business education. The repositioning proposed in this book is meant as a proposal to overcome this gap, taking organization design from a construct that is of little use in today's fast-moving technological, social and political environments to a new era dominated by ethical and aesthetic concerns. The repositioned framework changes the notion of organization design from one solely concerned with structure to one that compares design to a scaffold of meaning that supports every aspect of the organization's functioning. The scaffold is labeled *ethic-aesthetic* to reflect the primacy of values in organization design thinking and has a strong normative orientation although embracing also the ontological, cultural, as well as structural aspects of organization, as shown in Fig. 11.1.

In interpreting organization design as a perceptual, sensory and meaning-based phenomenon and in conceiving organization designing as something holistic, covering every corner of the organizational realm, an opportunity arises for the creation of a new managerial role. A role with moral and aesthetic obligations, in addition to the traditional performance-related responsibilities. To be sure, the organizational designer's role should be understood not as a post or function reserved for some managers, but as something of a *deontological nature*, embedded in regular managerial activity. Evidently, the competencies of the role are quite different from those of traditional managerial roles, and in addition to the typical rational-instrumental competencies, managers are required to build the aesthetic sensibility, which will give them the possibility to sense and evaluate the organization's ethic-aesthetic posture, as well as the organizational experiences of stakeholders. Such capabilities, which include a leadership component, materialize what Snow et al. (2005) have in mind, when these authors talk of organization design as a "meta-capability".

The need for more socially and environmentally responsible organizational/business outcomes has been expressed for years by MOS writers (see, for example, citation by Amis et al. 2021 at the outset). However, the weight of legacy, including various institutional, organizational and economic traditions, has perpetuated the status quo. And one of the key conditioning factors that can be singled out is the (scientific) tradition that has fuelled our MOS paradigm. Revision of this tradition is part of the mammoth task of reforming ***management education***, an undertaking that should not be postponed. Hence, once managers are taught about organization design not as hierarchical rules, but as a scaffold of morality, collaboration and purpose, things will begin to change, organizations will gradually become more humane and the aim of ***designing organizations for the betterment of society*** will no longer seem like a pipe dream.

References

Amis, J., S. Brickson, P. Haack, and M. Hernandez. 2021. Taking Inequality Seriously. *Academy of Management Review* 46 (3): 431–439.

Barnard, C.I. 1958. Elementary Conditions of Business Morals. *California Management Review* 1 (1): 1–13.

Dobson, J. 2022. Virtue Ethics, Aesthetics, and Reflective Practices in Business. *Philosophy of Management* 21: 493–505.

George, G., M.R. Haas, A.M. McGahan, S.J.D. Schillebeeckx, and P. Tracey. 2023. Purpose in the For-Profit Firm: A Review and Framework for Management Research. *Journal of Management* 49 (6): 1841–1869.

Hansen, H., A. Ropo, and E. Sauer. 2007. Aesthetic Leadership. *The Leadership Quarterly* 18: 544–560.

Krippendorff, K. 2006. *The Semantic Turn: A New Foundation for Design*. Boca Raton, FL: Taylor and Francis.

McKelvey, B. 1997. Perspective—Quasi-Natural Organization Science. *Organization Science* 8 (4): 351–380

Snow, C. C., Miles, R. E. & Miles, G. 2005. A configurational approach to the integration of strategy and organization research. *Strategic Organization*, 3 (4): 431–439

Index

R. Magalhães, *Designing Organizations for the Betterment of Society*, https://doi.org/10.1007/978-3-031-64483-2

I

K

L

M

N

O

The manufacturer's authorised representative in the EU is Springer Nature Customer Service Centre GmbH, Europaplatz 3, 69115 Heidelberg, Germany. If you have any concerns regarding our products, please contact ProductSafety@springernature.com

Printed and bound by CPI Group (UK) Ltd, Croydon, CR0 4YY

28/09/2026

02224083-0001